Nina is dedicated to living her life sold out to Christ. She is generally the first to volunteer and take risks for anything that grows the kingdom. She is always seeking to learn, develop, and cultivate herself in the integrity, character, fruit and will of God.

Connect with Nina and Manifold Grace Production Company and "Exercise to Life" at Manifoldgrace5@gmail.com, kingdomshifters.com or via Facebook, and Youtube.

Forward

My first encounter with the author Nina Cook was during her collegiate years where she attended a campus Bible Study I was leading. She was in a place of exploring what her destiny in life was and began to see where her passion for truth, calling to this generation, and gift of dance would all align to the apostolic mantle on her life. She would often release nuggets of mature wisdom and revelation that exceeded the realm of her peers and pierced generational expectation. In my six years of teaching college campus Bible study, it was a rare privilege to encounter such maturity, hunger and insight into the Apostolic which she has now captured with great strength and authority in her first book, **Apostolic Governing: Keys To Effectively Govern Your Destiny & Calling.**

Apostolic Governing *will accelerate your journey to destiny as you will find yourself in one of the 5 biblical characters' exploration. You cannot read this book and feel alone on your journey any longer. You will feel as if the author herself is walking out the journey with you, while giving you truths to stand and build upon. Each chapter challenges you to align or re-align with your destiny calling and be eternally transformed.*

Nina Cook's pioneering of Manifold Grace Dance Production has served as a launching pad for many who are called to the performing arts ministry and has helped them understand that their gifting and calling is strongly linked to their destiny in God. As she continues to dismantle and recreate what traditional church has viewed the place for the arts to operate in, she infuses and empowers others from an apostolic position. As you read this book you will not only gain knowledge but understand the heart of the author and the mandate on her life to see others walk in destiny.

Book Synopsis: *"Apostolic Governing: Keys To Effectively Govern Your Destiny & Calling" is a compilation of revelation, insight, and keys from five monumental people of the Bible, from the viewpoint of governing over who God destined and called them to be. Through biblical study this book reveals strategies and tools that are applicable in our lives today to reign victoriously in fulfilling our destiny, while towering over the assignments of the enemy against its fulfillment. It provides keys that we need to be responsible and accountable for what God has granted to our hands, and will shift you to valuing who God has ordained you to be. You will receive an impartation of knowledge and skills that will teach you how to fortify, protect, cover, and function as an apostolic governor over your destiny and calling.*

Apostolic Governing: Keys To Effectively Govern Your Destiny and Calling

(Website) Kingdomshifters.com

(Email) manifoldgrace5@gmail.com

Connect with Nina via Email, Facebook or YouTube

Copyright 2017 – Kingdom Shifters Ministries

All rights reserved. This book is protected by the copyright laws of the United States of America. This book may not be reprinted for commercial gain or profit. The use of occasional page copying for personal or group study is permitted and encouraged. Permission will be granted upon request.

Nina's Bio

Nina Cook has been saved since childhood and has been active in ministry much of her life. Nina carries an apostolic mantle with giftings in dance, singing, production, all manner of prayer, spiritual warfare, deliverance, healing, teaching, pastoring, scribing, and wellness. Nina graduated from Ball State University in 2014 with a Bachelor's Degree. She studied Exercise Science and minored in Dance. Nina has over five years of experience in the wellness and exercise field and 11 years and counting of dance experience.

Nina is an Elder at Kingdom Shifters Christian Empowerment Center in Muncie, Indiana. She is the main armor bearer for her pastor and is also training in her calling as an apostle. Nina is the founder of "Manifold Grace Production Company" and "Exercise to Life." It is her vision that her production company brings transformation to people and regions through the power and creativity of the arts. Nina is an extraordinary teacher and minister of movement, choreography, atmospheric worship, and using dance and movement in warfare and intercession. Nina provides fitness coaching and exercise and dance class through "Exercise to Life." She utilizes a vast variety of exercise and fitness styles that people can do that are combined with scriptural focuses, short teachings, prayers, and declarations and decrees such that when people do the exercises their bodies are transformed. It is her vision to see people transformed through bringing healing and deliverance to the physical body in areas that hinder their health and wellness, and to also see complete lifestyle changes that shift people into wholeness.

As a reader you can look forward to learning more about your true identity, a detailed study of the Word of God on the topic, and impactful reflective questions at the end of each chapter. Most importantly, you will learn how to not just hear or read about apostolic governing of your destiny and calling, but live it out daily! (Hint: Don't skip the bonus chapter!) My favorite chapter of the book is Chapter 4, as it encourages you to self-evaluate what standards God has called you to walk out in your life.

I decree everyone that reads this book will be eternally blessed with divine success of walking in their destiny daily!

Blessings,
Akeysha Headley
Faithwalk Harvest Center
Carpentersville, IL

Forward

"Apostolic Governing" provides strategic keys and insight into effectively governing your calling and destiny with continual success, upward motivation, and Godly momentum. I love how Nina uses her life experiences from childhood to present age and her journey into learning to apostolically govern her destiny to further bring the biblical revelation and strategies God is revealing to life. Her story demonstrates evidence that the keys work not only for biblical characters, but for any of us who wants to journey in fulfilled destiny with God, while being accountable to governing all he has granted to our hands.

The book also examines some of the challenges, trials, and negativities we will experience in destiny, how to embrace many of these challenges as part of your destinyo journey, and how to avoid unnecessary trials in our destiny walk. The biblical characters' lives and journeys are discussed in detail such that every key and strategy is unveiled for the purposes of equipping the reader with the tools essential to govern their relationship with God, govern different types of relationships with people, and to grow regardless of the people who are a part of their destiny journey in different seasons of their lives. This is essential as our relationship with God is the core of our destiny journey. People come and go, have many purposes, may not be able to handle the vision of our journey, can be hindrances to our destiny journey, etc. We must be able discern the difference and even if we were caught off guard, we must be able to forgive, heal, and keep pressing with God who is the most essential relationship of all. As long as we are aligned with him and connect in intimate relationship with him, we will have fulfilled relationships regardless to if they are for a season, lifetime, if people are for our destiny, or against it. "Apostolic Governing" increases your discernment and maturity in this area, and enables you to place relationships and situations in right perspective, and empowers you with tools to continue SHIFTING forward in the will, character, and ordained destiny of God.

A significant key this book reveals is knowing your enemy and the demons that will try to kill your destiny. Many Christians just start fighting with no insight or foresight when challenges arise. This book provides revelation to help you identify specific strongholds and demons assigned to the destiny of your calling and how to seek God for direction and keys to overthrow those demonic forces. This book is also balanced in revealing that every battle is not ours and how to discern when to fight, how to fight, what tools to fight with, and when to stay focus as sometimes the enemy is sending distractions to deter, alter, or hinder destiny. The chapters have questions and personal explorations and activations at the end of them, so you can strategically apply the knowledge learned to your daily destiny journey and see God's purpose effectively prevail in your life.

You must love the word to appreciate this book. The author utilizes in-depth scriptures to support the revelation and keys the Lord provides regarding governing destiny. The biblical study of each chapter is intense, refreshing, and mature. You will be SHIFTED to going beyond the written word, into the mysteries of the kingdom of heaven. If you are seeking to know the secrets to your destiny, then this book is for you.

I highly recommend "Apostolic Governing," and believe it will be life changing for anyone who desires strategic tools and revelation as they allow God to guide their destiny journey. Decreeing God's blessings and SHIFTING to healthy apostolic governing as you partake of the keys of this book and journey in a destiny lifestyle with God.

SHIFT!
Apostle Taquetta Baker
Founder of Kingdom Shifters Ministries
Muncie, Indiana

Table of Contents

From The Author Apostolic Governors Arise! 1

Chapter 1 Apostolic Governing Defined 6

    Chapter 1 Reflection Questions 21

Chapter 2 Nehemiah: The Apostolic Governor........ 22

    Part 1 Reflection Questions 47

    Part 2 Nehemiah: The Apostolic Governor 49

    Part 2 Reflection Questions 76

Chapter Mordecai & Esther: Apostolic Governing Covenant 78

Chapter 4 Samson: Opportunity Based Destiny vs. Lifestyle Based Destiny 119

    Chapter 4 Reflection Questions 146

Chapter 5 Daniel & His Companions: Excellent Servants Of God 147

    Part 1 Study Guide Questions.......................... 180

    Part 2 Daniel & His Companions: Excellent Servants Of God 181

    Part 2 Study Guide Questions.......................... 197

Chapter 6 Governing Yourself As The House Of The Lord 198

    Chapter 6 Reflection Questions 216

Chapter 7 Destiny As A Lifestyle 217

    Chapter 7 Reflection Questions 238

Chapter 8 My Destiny Fulfilled 240

From The Author Apostolic Governors Arise!

Initially, I did not plan to write a book. I was studying and journaling on Nehemiah and through his story, I was overwhelmed by how skillful he was in governing his calling. Through discernment, wisdom, prayer, and strategy, he overcame the enemy over and over again. As I read his story, revelation and insight began to flow. I realized that the knowledge I was gaining was applicable to my journey in the Lord, and that it needed to be shared.

Nehemiah's igniting story inspired me to study other books of the bible to continue learning about governing. Key after key became clear from reading stories like the need for constant prayer, being watchful of hidden plans of the enemy, being strategic in engaging warfare, and much more.

Some of them governed well and attained continual success, like Mordecai and Daniel, while others like Samson did not and failed miserably.

This is how this book was formed. It is a compilation of insight from the lives of specific monumental people of the Bible, on how they exercised godly skills to overcome the enemy and fulfill their calling. And while I was writing I was learning!

Thinking back over past experiences in my childhood, bullying was a constant challenge. One time at the end of a school day, a group of six classmates gave me a note that included a listing of all the things that each of them disliked about me, and why they did not want to be friends. This was a random happening and there were no altercations between us that warranted such a harmful note. Walking home from school I remember being hurt by their words and striving to figure out what I had done wrong. I wondered who I could share the note with and if they would be able to help me understand what I had done. I wanted to know if someone would be able to fix the situation for me and even tell me what I could do to change and be more accepted. Questions flooded my mind. Should I give the note to the teacher, my brother, my mother? Should I respond to the note and try to fix it, or tell them about themselves like they told me? I felt helpless in this moment, very alone, and confused. There was no one or nothing that could bring me clarity about this experience or explain to me why bullying was a continuous challenge for me. Returning to school the next day was difficult as I was still confused and embarrassed. The classmates who gave me the note ignored me for weeks until eventually the situation blew over. I never truly connected with them after this and although the situation blew over, the tension and the subtle bullying influence remained. I had a mentor and close friend that encouraged and helped me through the bullying altercations that proceeded through my elementary school years. I was glad when I found out I was attending a high school none of my classmates were going to. I did not endure bullying at my high school, but unfortunately, some of the challenges followed me to the dance school I joined in my neighborhood. I did not realize how deep the wounds of bullying impressed upon me. During my teenage years, which can sometimes already be difficult, the wounds began to express themselves. My family relationships were strained and drained, I experienced bouts of secret sadness and crying, my grades suffered and my passion for learning diminished. In the quiet storm, I was trying to find peace and comfort within myself despite everything that strived to persuade me that something was wrong with me. As I progressed through high school, dance became my outlet and hiding place. My focus was set on pursuing a career and future in dance. Senior year, I was accepted into the dance program at Ball State University and my life dramatically changed in college. **God's call strongly** drew me, so I committed to a deeper wholly devoted relationship with him and I accepted the call on my life. I attended weekly bible study, joined a church in the community, and began to explore the use of my gift of dance for ministry. Through my college experience, the challenges of bullying did not continue. My relationships comprised of those who were of like faith, which made them healthy and beneficial to what God was doing in my life and where he was taking me. Mentors and spiritual leaders drew to me as they noticed my calling and desire for destiny. Their guidance taught me about how to navigate through a life in the Lord and they began to build skills in me such that I could maintain and soar in destiny. Prayer, journaling, worship, consistent devotional time with the Lord, and study of the scripture all became embedded disciplines of my everyday lifestyle. My entire life became about walking in God's destiny for me and fulfilling my purpose. Later in my destiny journey, God revealed to me that his call was on my life from an early age and I was destined to be a giant killer- one who towers over and demolishes demonic principalities, powers, and ruler spirits that seek to assert rule over people and regions. I was drawn to the story of David and Goliath where God taught me one of the principalities I was called to combat was the spirit of Goliath; the bully who taunted the Israelites and defied God. Finally, something explained my continuous experiences with bullying. The enemy saw who I was called to be and wanted to distort me such that I would not boldly fight against Goliath and the other principalities and powers I would encounter later in life as my calling and destiny unfolded. Through bullying, the enemy tried to plant seeds of fear, intimidation, and low self-esteem, such that my identity would be too damaged, and wounded to govern adequately who I was destined to be. Therefore, after receiving this revelation from God I understand the need for governing over our destinies and callings, and being taught this from an early age.

This is needed because:

- ✓ Your personal identity will give you revelation about how the enemy will aim to attack you
- ✓ It will aid you in alleviating seeds that the enemy tries to plant in your journey to hinder its fulfillment

- ✓ It will teach you about how to be responsible for who you are in the Lord and value it
- ✓ The revelation will increase your knowledge of effective prayer skills, the importance of discernment, wisdom, having vision, governing relationships, being devoted to serving the Lord and his standards for your life, embodying a spirit of excellence, and strategic tactics to dismantle the attacks of the enemy
- ✓ It is an essential part of the lifestyle of one who walks successfully in destiny and calling

This book will serve as a foundation that will give you keys to assist you in beginning your new lifestyle as an apostolic governor of who God has destined and called you to be.

Apostolic governors arise!

Chapter 1
Apostolic Governing Defined

<u>*Governance*</u> from Dictionary.com means:

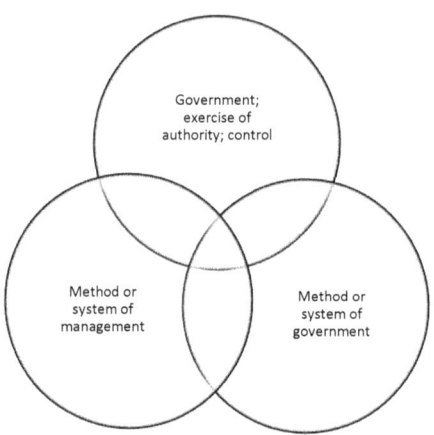

<u>*Govern*</u> from Dictionary.com means:

1. To rule over by right of authority
2. To exercise a directing or restraining influence over; guide
3. To hold in check; control
4. To serve as or constitute a law for
5. To be regularly accompanied by or require the use of
6. To regulate the speed
7. To exercise the function of government
8. To have predominating influence

Apostolic governance is the strategic application of the authority, rule, and power of God over a specific assignment, group of people, region, and nation. Each assignment is an exercise in the fulfillment of your destiny. In implementing these strategies, you guard and protect your destiny and calling from the wiles of the enemy that are sent against the development and fruition of it. Apostolic governing is not only a set of leadership skills that are used in an assignment, but is a force for regulating personal choices.

Apostolic governing is essential to our authenticity because if it is not protected it can be easily thwarted and destroyed by the enemy. If the enemy hinders what we have been called to do, it will affect those who were to receive of our fruit.

Being an apostolic governor is like being the watchmen over your own destiny.

> ***Isaiah 62:6-7*** *I have set watchmen upon thy walls, O Jerusalem, which shall never hold their peace day nor night: ye that make mention of the Lord, keep not silence, And give him no rest, till he establish, and till he make Jerusalem a praise in the earth.*

Set in the Strong's concordance in this scripture means to appoint, to attend to, make overseer, to entrust, governor, ruler. As watchmen, we have an assignment to keep, preserve, and protect which means (1) to be one's guard, take heed, take care, beware, (2) to keep oneself, retain, abstain, and (3) to pay keep, to keep oneself from.

God appoints us to be the governor over our own destiny and calling. He entrusted us with the office to attend to the deposit that he has placed in us.

As watchman, we have 5 distinct levels of responsibility:

- Protect ourselves such that lives are saved and impacted by what God has planted in us.
- Keep and restrain ourselves within the bounds, principles, and practices of God that are profitable to our destiny and calling.
- Abstain and keep ourselves away from sin, unhealthiness, and issues that would be destructive to our destiny and calling.
- Govern our lives by our covenant relationship with the Lord, following and walking in his commandments, vows, and standards
- Beware, cautious, and careful of things that would be a deterrence in our destiny and calling.

As apostolic governors, these practices are to be enmeshed within the daily walk of our destiny and calling because they are what protect it from being interfered with by the enemy. The scripture says, "I have set watchman upon thy walls, O Jerusalem, which shall never hold their peace day nor night." One of the definitions of *never* in the Strong's concordance in this scripture is continual employment. It is our job to keep watch and govern over our destiny. At any regular job, if we do not put in the work, we will not progress in our tasks, and we will not get paid. It is the same in our spiritual employment. If we do not complete the work we will not fulfill our God-ordained assignments, and we will not reap any benefits or rewards from it. It is a job uniquely assigned to us, so only we can do it. We are hand-picked by God no matter the present circumstance of our lives.

Governing is a continual work and journey. Through the journey, we increase and become mantled with the skills that assist us in the process. We are more often taught about our gifts alone. Many have come into embracing their gifts and destiny, but are not taught about how to effectively govern in destiny to maintain within the journey throughout their lives into completion. They are also not equipped to deal with the assignments set against them, thus they succumb to warfare and traps that the enemy inevitably sets for those who walk in their purpose.

Teaching and equipping is needed because too many destinies are being stolen by the enemy. Many have not consistently progressed in their calling, and we rarely see what true sustainability and completion of destiny and calling entails. We scarcely see generational spiritual lineage, successorship, and the passing of mantles because many mantles are dropping before they can be passed. Some are dying with the mantle due to never truly sowing into and raising up others. As those arising to begin a new journey of walking in destiny and calling or those who have already been treading this destiny journey, the world needs you to govern what God has planted in you sufficiently such that it can be completely fulfilled and even carried on for generations to come.

In Matthew 25:14-28, there is a story of a man going on a journey. He called his servants and entrusted them with some of his property. He gave each servant the number of talents that he felt matched their ability. Through this we learn that God entrusts us with what he knows is within our capability. The one who was given five produced five more, the one given two produced two more, but the one who received one dug a hole and hid the talent. The man came back to collect the talents and was pleased with the ones who produced something from the talents, and rewarded them with an increase of responsibility. On the other hand, for the one who hid his talent, God was displeased and took from him the talent that he did have. This parable is representative of being able to govern effectively over what God entrusts to us. This is not to say that God will strip us of our calling the first time we make a mistake. God has planted in us all that we need to flourish, but it is what we do with his **investment** that will determine our product.

The parable reveals:

- Those who invest in destiny and calling, and those who just hold the calling and never invest in it
- Those who produce fruit from what God has given them, and those who do not
- Those who know how to grow, increase, and expand in what God has given them, and those who stay stagnant thus, losing what they have

- Those who are faithful servants over their destiny and calling, and those who are unfaithful and do not serve.
- Those who are fearful of investing, and those who are fearless to sow into what God has given them

God has given me a fine arts production company called Manifold Grace. We are a company that utilizes various forms of the arts (dance, music, song, visual art, poetry, drama) to spread the word and will of God while bringing deliverance, healing, and miracles to people, organizations, communities and regions. Ministering through the multifaceted grace of God, we execute skilled keen movement and words from the Lord to shift atmospheres and establish God's kingdom in the earth.

Every year God plants a new revelation within my spirit regarding the focus of the production, and each time there is an elevation. The lighting, set decorations, garments, choreography, poetry all increase to new levels.

I spend my time:

- Praying into the vision and for all team members- this fortifies us in the word and what God is speaking to us for the production. It also builds us in our power, authority, confidence, and boldness
- Fasting and increased exercise- this is time for consecrating with God and communing with His spirit. It is also time for strengthening,

- training, and disciplining my body so that it can sustain through the rigors of the production
- Seeking God for choreography that is truly impactful- movement that embodies his word, shifts atmospheres, people and regions, administrates healing, deliverance, miracles, empowerment and breakthrough, and brings heaven to earth so that tangible fruit is produced
- Envisioning the stage setup and decorations- When God gave me the vision of the production he gave clear instructions that the service must be a production and not a church service. So it is important that I do not settle for the familiar, be creative, and think outside of the box. I take the time to envision and put together a set that visually displays the theme God has given for the production
- Connecting with those who are gifted in other art forms- this allows the company to connect with other ministries, draw other artists who are gifted but may not have the opportunity to utilize their gifts for God, and a chance to receive new company members
- Sowing money into dance garments because this is a part of the covering, identity, and presentation of the ministry
- Wholeheartedly giving of my time and focus.

My investment is spending my time both spiritually and naturally cultivating the vision, which allows God to increase his revelation and anointing upon my life and the vision of the production and company. As I take my time to sow into what God has granted to my hands I learn more, am able to bring my skill into greater excellence, and produce tangible fruit from the ministry. My governing gives a model to those who are a part of the company and demonstrates the importance of sowing into who they are as ministers of the company, and their own personal unique gifts and calling. As they build themselves up personally, they have a better revelation of who they are in God and their purpose in the company which takes the entire team to a new level of excellence and fruitfulness.

How do you invest in what God has placed in you?

The scripture says, "For to everyone who has will more be given, and he will have an abundance. But from the one who has not, even what he has will be taken away." God has invested into all of us what we need to be fruitful in destiny and calling. How we invest and govern over ourselves will determine our success.

Invest from Dictionary.com means

1. To use, give, or devote (time, talent, etc.) as for a purpose to achieve something
2. To furnish with power, authority, rank, etc.
3. To furnish or endow with power, right, etc., vest
4. To endow with a quality or characteristic
5. To infuse or belong to, as a quality or characteristic

6. To install in an office or position
7. To clothe, attire, dress
8. To surround by military forces or works so as to prevent, approach or escape; besiege

When we invest in our destiny and calling we are devoting time to learning, becoming a student of our destiny. We are furnished with power, authority, rank, and character to walk in it effectively and clothed with what we need to achieve. We are being guarded by military forces of God to prevent the enemy from infiltrating it. Learning how to apostolically govern our lives is a part of how we adequately invest in our "talents", and is the way to which we will hear "Well done, good and faithful servant. You have been faithful over a little; I will set you over much. Enter into the joy of your master."

Many times, we give this job to God and entrust the fulfillment of our calling to God, and we do it without any personal ownership and responsibility, when he has given us the power, authority, and skills to be able to watch over and guard over our own callings. God is very well capable of governing us alone, but that is not his design; he has entrusted the governing ability to us.

There have been instances where I have faced challenges that were a part of the development of my apostolic calling. I would have understanding of its purpose, but I would do nothing about it. It was great to have understanding, but with being action-less I was not receiving the training God was taking me through. I was not learning and being equipped in my identity to overcome the challenges I was facing. I came to the realization that if I did not step forward and take responsibility of my own calling I would not grow into the fullness of who God had ordained me to be.

I would often have dreams where dark demonic figures would be chasing me and each time I would take off running. Sometimes I could fly, but I would only fly a little before falling back to the ground continuing to run, then eventually waking up. God was trying to teach me how to operate inside of the spirit realm and that I had the power to fight these demonic figures using my spiritual weapons. Flying in the dream also meant that I had the ability to tower and soar over these demonic figures. Yet, each time I was brought onto the training ground while asleep, I would run and could not sustain in flying. Finally, I came to the realization that just going to sleep at night not doing anything, hoping I would have a different dream was not the solution. I began to pray for my spirit man to be awake, alert and empowered to fight before I went to bed. My spiritual mother would pray for me and impart her knowledge on night season spiritual warfare. In my prayer time during the day, I would pray about my dreams and spend time cleansing fear while filling myself with the revelation and truth of the power and weapons that I had access to in the spirit realm while both sleep and awake. Immediate fruit was produced as I fortified myself, and my night season was changed tremendously. Now I punch, kick, shoot, slice, fight, soar flying way up high into different realms while I am sleeping.

Sometimes I chase the demons and have them running on top of cars for shelter. I took charge and began to govern this spiritual training process through investing myself with prayer, knowledge, and empowerment. Fervent prayer, decreeing and declaring out who I was, studying and building myself up in the word, all became tools I utilized to take ownership of my destiny and calling and I began to be more victorious as I applied these skills. We must gain interest from God's investment in us.

> *Luke 10:19 Behold, I give unto you power to tread on serpents and scorpions, and over all the power of the enemy: and nothing shall by any means hurt you.*

- ✓ The power to crush all of our enemies without being harmed

> *Luke 24:29 And, behold, I send the promise of my Father upon you: but tarry ye in the city of Jerusalem, until ye be endued with power from on high.*

- ✓ We have been endued and clothed with power from on high

> *1 Peter 5:8 Be sober, be vigilant; because your adversary the devil, as a roaring lion, walketh about, seeking whom he may devour:*

- ✓ We are told to be watchful and alert because the devil is seeking for ways to devour us

> *2 Timothy 1:7 For God hath not given us the spirit of fear; but of power, and of love, and of a sound mind.*

- ✓ We have been given attributes of God for effective balanced governing. No fear, but power, love, and the soundness of our minds

***Philippians 4:13** I can do all things through Christ which strengtheneth me.*

- ✓ We have the strength to do all things

***Acts 1:8** But ye shall receive power, after that the Holy Ghost is come upon you: and ye shall be witnesses unto me both in Jerusalem, and in all Judaea, and in Samaria, and unto the uttermost part of the earth.*

- ✓ We have received the promise of the Holy Spirit- Gods spirit empowering us

***Genesis 1:26 And** God said, Let us make man in our image, after our likeness: and let them have dominion over the fish of the sea, and over the fowl of the air, and over the cattle, and over all the earth, and over every creeping thing that creepeth upon the earth.*

- ✓ We have been created in the image of God, thus we have his nature and genes
- ✓ Dominion and governing rule has been given to us

From the beginning of our creation God has given us dominion. This means that the governing part of our spiritual DNA has remained dormant if we are not operating in our God-given jurisdiction. We have been underdeveloped, and have lived below the means of our power. It is like superman never knowing he could fly. He would still be able to win every battle, but would have fought from the ground rather than from the sky- the height of his capacity. We must be developed to carry the call, be mature in it, operate in its full capacity, and arise in the dormant places. He has given us the keys of the kingdom of heaven; these are governing keys.

> ***Matthew 16:19*** *And I will give unto thee the keys of the kingdom of heaven: and whatsoever thou shalt bind on earth shall be bound in heaven: and whatsoever thou shalt loose on earth shall be loosed in heaven.*

<u>*Keys* in the Strong's in the scripture means:</u>

1. a key- since the keeper of the keys has the power to open and to shut
2. to denote power and authority of various kinds

This is implication that we have been granted limitless governing ability in both heaven and on earth- in the spirit realm (supernatural), and in the natural realm (earth). It is not just one key, but we have been given multiple keys.

Through apostolic governing we gain the keys of:

- Having enlightened spiritual senses such that we can see and hear the attacks of the enemy before they come
- Heightened discernment abilities to identify the hidden plans of the enemy, the difference between God's voice and the devils. The ability to recognize when someone or something is being used against us, and how to determine real warfare from unnecessary warfare

- Strategic prayer weapons and strategies against the enemy
- How to remain hidden and under the radar from the enemy
- How to maneuver strategically and conquer through different types of demonic warfare tactics
- Being consistent in praying and seeking the Lord for his divine downloads and instruction from heaven to walk successfully in destiny, calling, and fulfilling various assignments
- Being an effective vision leader and one who God will use to govern those who are carriers of the vision with them
- Walking in the spirit of excellence with a heart to always please the Lord
- Shifting people, regions, territories, and nations to embody the will, nature, and culture of God

All the keys that we receive through apostolic governing chisel and shape us in the wholeness of our God-ordained destiny, calling, and image. Apostolic governing aims to preserve and protect us in the rawest and purest form without demonic deposits that alter and tear away from the fullness of who God has called us to be and the fullness that is to be birthed from the womb of it.

Prayer:

Decreeing a shift is taking place in you and you are taking the full ownership and responsibility of your destiny and calling. No longer are you putting on God what he has granted to your hands. You are being activated as the watchman of your destiny and being freshly mantled with power and authority to be effective and successful in the position. You will not operate below your means because you are shifting to becoming an investor of your own destiny and calling. Decreeing that you will take the time to cultivate and develop what God has granted to your hands and become a student of your destiny. Decreeing you will have a zeal to pray, to seek God, to study his word, and you will have an urgency upon you to implement what he reveals to you is necessary for who you are. You will fly and you will soar in the fullness of your capacity as God continually expands you in your destiny journey. In Jesus name, Amen.

Chapter 1
Reflection Questions

1. *Review the 5 distinct level of responsibility listed in this chapter. Search out how well you believe you do in each of the listed areas, and where you feel you can improve.*

2. *What has God invested in you? If you do not know spend time in prayer asking God to reveal it to you.*

3. *In what ways do you invest in your destiny and calling? How can you improve in this?*

4. *How can you take more personal ownership and responsibility for your destiny and calling?*

5. *Are there areas where you know you are operating below the means of who God has called you to be?*

Chapter 2
Nehemiah: The Apostolic Governor

Nehemiah is an Old Testament apostle who operated in apostolic governing. We will look at this chapter of the Bible to receive specific keys about apostolic governance and its importance as we walk in our destiny, calling, and fulfill the assignments of the Lord on our lives.

> ***Nehemiah 1:1-4 English Standard Version*** *The words of Nehemiah the son of Hacaliah. Now it happened in the month of Chislev, in the twentieth year, as I was in Susa the citadel, that Hanani, one of my brothers, came with certain men from Judah. And I asked them concerning the Jews who escaped, who had survived the exile, and concerning Jerusalem. And they said to me, "The remnant there in the province who had survived the exile is in great trouble and shame. The wall of Jerusalem is broken down, and its gates are destroyed by fire." As soon as I heard these words I sat down and wept and mourned for days, and I continued fasting and praying before the God of heaven.*

In this passage, Nehemiah is told about the condition of Jerusalem and the people left there. The wall of Jerusalem had been broken down, and the gates of the city had also been burned. When Nehemiah heard the news, he was grieved and began to fast and pray for days. He went into an instant state of intercession and sought the face of Lord, rather than becoming wrapped up in grief and overcome by his emotions.

His emotions, grief, and passion pushed him into action to receive results and solutions to the problem.

You will be faced with terrible challenges and tragic situations as you walk in your destiny and calling, but it is essential to not get wrapped up in your emotions. Allow them to propel you into action- to pray, fast, intercede, and seek the Lord for results and solutions to the situations placed before you. Apostolic governors are solution seekers and are positioned before the Lord to be the answer. They have the heart and compassion of the Lord and are focused in prayer to receive his divine instruction on how to change situations and produce results.

> ***Nehemiah 1:5-11 English Standard Version*** *And I said, "O Lord God of heaven, the great and awesome God who keeps covenant and steadfast love with those who love him and keep his commandments, let your ear be attentive and your eyes open, to hear the prayer of your servant that I now pray before you day and night for the people of Israel your servants, confessing the sins of the people of Israel, which we have sinned against you. Even I and my father's house have sinned. We have acted very corruptly against you and have not kept the commandments, the statutes, and the rules that you commanded your servant Moses. Remember the word that you commanded your servant Moses, saying, 'If you are unfaithful, I will scatter you among the peoples, but if you return to me and keep my commandments and do them, though your outcasts are in the uttermost parts of heaven, from there I will gather them and bring them to the place*

> *that I have chosen, to make my name dwell there.' They are your servants and your people, whom you have redeemed by your great power and by your strong hand. O Lord, let your ear be attentive to the prayer of your servant, and to the prayer of your servants who delight to fear your name, and give success to your servant today, and grant him mercy in the sight of this man." Now I was cupbearer to the king.*

Nehemiah stood in intercession for the people and repented for their sins, his sins, and the sins of his lineage. He acknowledged the wrongdoings of both himself, and the people toward God. His prayer was from a broken and contrite heart, therefore, God could not despise him (Psalm 51:17). He brought spiritual restoration between himself, the people, and God before he could go forward in the natural restoration of rebuilding the wall and city. True restoration could not occur if covenant relationship and right standing with God was not first rebuilt. Had he built before restoring, the walls and gates would have come tumbling right back down because the root issues were not dealt with. The ruined condition of Jerusalem was symbolic of its spiritual state and covenant with God that had to be restored first before it could be manifested in the natural realm.

Apostolic governors are willing to repent personally and on behalf of others, which is a display of mature character. When they go forward in their calling and assignments, they are not cocky and arrogant- blaming everything on people or the devil. They willingly acknowledge all wrongdoing and disobedience that may be present within themselves. Because of this, God hears their prayers, answers them, and grants favor to them. They go beyond the surface and identify the roots of the situations and challenges that are placed before them. What they build stands because they produce deep healing, deliverance, and restoration. They build in the spirit realm first, and then they translate what is built in the spirit into the natural to benefit people, regions, and nations.

While Nehemiah was serving King Artaxerxes (king of Babylon), the king noticed his sadness and expressed concern.

> ***Nehemiah 2:5-8 English Standard Version*** *And I said to the king, "If it pleases the king, and if your servant has found favor in your sight, that you send me to Judah, to the city of my fathers' graves, that I may rebuild it." And the king said to me (the queen sitting beside him), "How long will you be gone, and when will you return?" So it pleased the king to send me when I had given him a time. And I said to the king, "If it pleases the king, let letters be given me to the governors of the province Beyond the River, that they may let me pass through until I come to Judah, and a letter to Asaph, the keeper of the king's forest, that he may give me timber to make beams for the gates of the fortress of the temple, and for the wall of the city, and for the house that I shall occupy." And the king granted me what I asked, for the good hand of my God was upon me.*

Nehemiah tells the King of his desire to go and rebuild the wall of Jerusalem and his request is granted. He received multiple letters from the king to cover his contact with other men of authority, e.g. the keeper of the forest, other governors, and to be given the supplies he needed for building. He had a well-conceived plan. He knew what he would need from the officials and the supplies he needed to build. Nehemiah's letters from the king granted him legal authority and jurisdiction to build in the region.

Apostolic governors understand the need for truly being sent by God to do a work, and the importance of attaining his legal authority to function. They know they cannot just show up in a region and start building using their resources. God's legal jurisdictional power upon them will enable them to find favor within their regions, communities, and nations to complete their assignment. They will have clear vision of the resources they need, and will be bold in asking the Lord for it. They are not afraid to pray (ask, seek, knock) for what they need in order to effectively execute the assignment.

> *Nehemiah 2:11-16 English Standard Version So I went to Jerusalem and was there three days. Then I arose in the night, I and a few men with me. And I told no one what my God had put into my heart to do for Jerusalem. There was no animal with me but the one on which I rode. I went out by night by the Valley Gate to the Dragon Spring and to the Dung Gate, and I inspected the walls of Jerusalem that were broken down and its gates that had been destroyed by fire. Then I went on to the Fountain*

> Gate and to the King's Pool, but there was no room for the animal that was under me to pass. Then I went up in the night by the valley and inspected the wall, and I turned back and entered by the Valley Gate, and so returned. And the officials did not know where I had gone or what I was doing, and I had not yet told the Jews, the priests, the nobles, the officials, and the rest who were to do the work.

Nehemiah went to the site of his assignment to examine the land and gates of the city to evaluate its current state. He strategically stayed hidden and under the radar from the enemy gaining insight and knowledge of his plan before it was time by going out during the night to inspect the land. The scripture says he viewed the wall.

View in the Strong's in this scripture means:

1. to scrutinize, by implication of watching
2. to expect with hope and patience
3. hope, tarry, view
4. wait, to inspect, examine

As he viewed the place of his assignment it was as if he was waiting to hear from the Lord on how to begin building. He was positioned in hope, patience, and expectation to receive a divine download from heaven about how to go forward in rebuilding. His natural eyes were inspecting while his supernatural eyes were simultaneously gaining God's vision for the assignment.

Even though we may receive assignments from the Lord that we are passionate about, we must be patient before taking action on the assignment. We cannot just go out on a whim, running on passion, intellect, and plans that have worked in the past that are not specific to the occasion. We also cannot take quick action based on need, as the people of the city needed to be restored. We have to wait and be led by the Lord, and receive wise direction and vision downloads from Him that are specific to the assignment to fulfill it by His design.

Nehemiah could have looked at the land and immediately said "Okay I see how I can do this; let's get started now." He didn't rush, he waited patiently on the Lord. Apostolic governors must do the same.

By Nehemiah going to the very territory of the assignment, he claimed and gained ownership over that land in the spirit realm. He visited the gates and claimed them, becoming established as a gatekeeper. Joshua 1:3 says "Every place that the sole of your foot shall tread upon, that have I given unto you, as I said unto Moses." Nehemiah treaded on the land and gained dominion to go forward in the will of the Lord to restore the city. Apostolic governors gain dominion when they tread upon the regions and territories that they are called to govern. They become established as gatekeepers who can govern over what comes in and what goes out, what operates and does not operate, what is produced and what is not produced.

As Nehemiah visited the city he was strategic because he went and did not tell anyone what he was doing. He did not risk prematurely releasing what God was leading him to do to others- not even the people of the land who were affected by the poor condition of the city. As even in telling them about it, they could have sabotaged his assignment. They could have been doubtful, discouraged, depressed, and even used as betrayers and back stabbers to the fulfilling of the assignment. He avoided interference because he was strategic in his ability to discern the timing of releasing the knowledge and revelation about the plans of God that were about to take place. He did not even tell the few men that were with him, as they could have begun to speak out of negativity, disbelief, and bitterness and cursed the work before it even got started.

Apostolic governors must discern the timing of the Lord for when to release to others the plans of the assignment. Even close friends, family, and ministry team members can be detrimental to the work if they are told the plan prematurely because they do not have the capacity to receive, comprehend, and become a part of the fruition of the vision at that time. We have to hold the vision until the appointed time of God to release it such that we do not cause the assignment to be aborted. There have been times I wanted to share with people outside of my spiritual family that God was shaping me as a young apostle, but God would not let me. The desire to share was from a place of wanting their support and encouragement, but God revealed that sharing prematurely would open up doors to unnecessary warfare, negativity, and word curses from those who did not agree or understand his plan for me. This was a time to be hidden in him and allow the fruit to speak for itself in its season.

God placed the assignment upon Nehemiah, so for the time being he had to be the one to carry it alone. His feet had to tread upon the region, his eyes had to inspect the ruin, and he had to receive the supernatural download from heaven on how to build and restore. Apostolic governors have to be okay with carrying the vision alone until God releases others who have the capacity and design to be vision carriers. Not everybody's womb can carry and birth forth the vision God has given you. We have to be careful about who we plant the seed of the vision in so that it is not aborted or distorted. We have to be hands on and active in the work, and know that even though we may have vision carriers, we are going to be the main recipient of the vision.

> *Nehemiah 2:17-20 English Standard Version*
> *Then I said to them, "You see the trouble we are in, how Jerusalem lies in ruins with its gates burned. Come, let us build the wall of Jerusalem, that we may no longer suffer derision." And I told them of the hand of my God that had been upon me for good, and also of the words that the king had spoken to me. And they said, "Let us rise up and build." So they strengthened their hands for the good work. But when Sanballat the Horonite and Tobiah the Ammonite servant and Geshem the Arab heard of it, they jeered at us and despised us and said, "What is this thing that you are doing? Are you rebelling against the king?" Then I replied to them, "The God of heaven will make us prosper, and we his servants*

will arise and build, but you have no portion or right or claim in Jerusalem."

Since Nehemiah gained jurisdiction in Jerusalem both naturally and spiritually there was nothing that the people or the kings and nobles in high places could do to hinder the transference of his spiritual ownership into natural ownership and authority to begin rebuilding the wall and restoring the land. He had good favor with the Lord, so the people of Jerusalem agreed with the work and became capable vision carriers as the scripture says "so they strengthened their hands for this good work." They became equipped and empowered to be a part of the assignment.

Sanballat, Tobiah, and Geshem mocked the assignment but their negativity and scorn fell on hollow ground. There was nothing that the devil could do about it. They tried to pin rebellion on Nehemiah, but he responded by way of decree, "The God of heaven, he will prosper us; therefore we his servants will arise and build: but ye have no portion, nor right, nor memorial in Jerusalem".

He could not be denied as he had full jurisdiction and decreed out to them that they had no right or portion. His decree showed he was confident and sure in the Lord and his assignment.

Apostolic governors cannot be denied when they have full jurisdiction over what they are called to do. They know how to maneuver to remain hidden from the enemy as they do strategic work within the assignment. They are skilled in their ability to transfer their spiritual authority and ownership into the natural realm as they go forward in fulfilling their assignments. They know that once they have established things within the spirit realm, and have received divine instruction and endowment from the Lord, nothing that the enemy releases against them will prosper. Apostolic governors must be confident in this, and cannot waver or move from this stance when difficulties and challenges- which have no power- are thrown at them. Apostolic governors recognize that what the enemy speaks against them is only an illusion and trick to get them to respond and move from their stance. WE ARE NOT FOOLED! WE SEE YOU, DEVIL!

> ***Nehemiah 3:1-6 English Standard Version*** *Then Eliashib the high priest rose up with his brothers the priests, and they built the Sheep Gate. They consecrated it and set its doors. They consecrated it as far as the Tower of the Hundred, as far as the Tower of Hananel. And next to him the men of Jericho built. And next to them Zaccur the son of Imri built.*
>
> *The sons of Hassenaah built the Fish Gate. They laid its beams and set its doors, its bolts, and its bars. And next to them Meremoth the son of Uriah, son of Hakkoz repaired. And next to them Meshullam the son of Berechiah, son of Meshezabel repaired. And next to them Zadok the son of Baana repaired. And next to them the Tekoites repaired, but their nobles would not stoop to serve their Lord. Joiada the son of Paseah and Meshullam the son of*

> *Besodeiah repaired the Gate of Yeshanah. They laid its beams and set its doors, its bolts, and its bars.*

Nehemiah was able to position each person in their spot on the wall right where they needed to be and where they had the skill to build. He apostolically delegated over the assignment. This entire chapter of Nehemiah is a listing of all of the people who were working on rebuilding the wall and city. The entire wall and city were full of people, and there was no work going undone, no arguments and drama breaking out, no challenges and issues amongst the people. Everyone was focused on working and completing their delegated task.

Apostolic governors recognize the skill of each person and place them accordingly where their skills and gifts will be most effective and fruitful in completing the assignment. They are team builders, community makers, and unity establishers.

> ***Nehemiah 4:1-6 English Standard Version*** *Now when Sanballat heard that we were building the wall, he was angry and greatly enraged, and he jeered at the Jews. And he said in the presence of his brothers and of the army of Samaria, "What are these feeble Jews doing? Will they restore it for themselves? Will they sacrifice? Will they finish up in a day? Will they revive the stones out of the heaps of rubbish, and burned ones at that?" Tobiah the Ammonite was beside him, and he said, "Yes, what they are building – if a fox goes up on it he will break down their stone wall!" Hear, O our God, for we are despised. Turn back their taunt on their*

> *own heads and give them up to be plundered in a land where they are captives. Do not cover their guilt, and let not their sin be blotted out from your sight, for they have provoked you to anger in the presence of the builders. So we built the wall. And all the wall was joined together to half its height, for the people had a mind to work.*

Constant opposition and negativity was being released against Nehemiah and the workers as they worked on the wall. They were being mocked, taunted, and despised but Nehemiah remained focused on the work and persevered in prayer. Sanballat and Tobiah were naysayers releasing fiery darts against the work that was going forth, but Nehemiah was not moved. He dealt with things in the spirit realm through prayer. "Turn back their taunt on their own heads and give them up to be plundered in a land where they are captives." He prayed a **boomerang prayer**, such that the words and taunts of the naysayers and mockers would turn back onto them. He prayed, "Do not cover their guilt, and let not their sin be blotted out from your sight, for they have provoked you to anger in the presence of the builders." This was a **prayer of judgment**, that the anger of the Lord would be released against them. Apostolic governors know how to utilize the various forms of prayer weapons, and they are skilled in executing them against the enemy. At a previous job, an opportunity for a promotion opened and I applied immediately. I was prayerful that the job was already mine. My supervisors interviewed me and felt that I would not be able to handle the job because I had not worked with the company for multiple years. Although excelling above the rest, teaching others, and troubleshooting problems quickly became some of attributes I was known for within the office. My supervisors did not seem to take my excellent work ethic into account and were demeaning in their dialogue with me concerning the position. Confronting them head on about this would have increased my warfare and was not wise. Therefore, I skillfully took my prayers to the Lord. God told me that this was my season of job promotion and to stay focused in standing strong in his word as my truth. A few months passed, and God opened a door for me with another company. It was a job of higher pay and greater advancement, so I excitedly took the position and knew that God had answered my prayers. Those prayers helped me to conquer over the hindering words of the naysayers such that I could walk in the manifestation of God's plan and blessing for me. Skillful prayers against your naysayers will be effectual.

Nehemiah knew that the weapons of his warfare were not carnal, but they were mighty through God (2 Corinthians 10:4). Although Sanballat and Tobiah were releasing carnal words and taunts, Nehemiah did not respond from the carnal realm. He knew that the fight was really taking place in the spirit realm, so he dealt with resistance from that place. That made his weapons all the more overpowering in relations to the weapons that were against him. As while they were throwing carnal darts, he was throwing spiritual darts, godly judgment, and boomerang prayers!

Apostolic governors know where the fight is. They do not waste time- fighting useless carnal battles with people and the devil. They deal with things in the spirit realm swiftly, fiercely, boldly, and fearlessly. They are not afraid to stand toe to toe with the devil and demonic principalities on assignment against the work. They know the power of God that is with them and the power of their weapons.

Nehemiah 4:6 says, "So we built the wall. And all the wall was joined together to half its height, for the people had a mind to work." Even through all of the warfare the work was not deterred. While prayer was going forth in the spirit realm and the spiritual weapons were dismantling the works of the enemy, the people continued to have a mind to work. Through the mocking, taunting, and variations of warfare, the vision carriers will keep going forward. They will have the spirit of the leader, and a spirit for the completion of the assignment. Even through times of engaging in intense warfare, the work will not cease to flourish.

> *2 Corinthians 10:4 For the weapons of our warfare are not carnal, but mighty through God to the pulling down of strong holds.*

> *Nehemiah 4:7-14 English Standard Version But when Sanballat and Tobiah and the Arabs and the Ammonites and the Ashdodites heard that the repairing of the walls of Jerusalem was going forward and that the breaches were beginning to be closed, they were very angry. And they all plotted together to come and fight against Jerusalem and to*

cause confusion in it. And we prayed to our God and set a guard as a protection against them day and night. In Judah it was said, "The strength of those who bear the burdens is failing. There is too much rubble. By ourselves we will not be able to rebuild the wall." And our enemies said, "They will not know or see till we come among them and kill them and stop the work." At that time the Jews who lived near them came from all directions and said to us ten times, "You must return to us." So in the lowest parts of the space behind the wall, in open places, I stationed the people by their clans, with their swords, their spears, and their bows. And I looked and arose and said to the nobles and to the officials and to the rest of the people, "Do not be afraid of them. Remember the Lord, who is great and awesome, and fight for your brothers, your sons, your daughters, your wives, and your homes."

The naysayers heard that the repairing of the wall was going forward and that the breaches were being closed so they were angry. The enemy began to recognize the success of the work and that it was getting closer to being fulfilled. His openings for demonic infiltration were closing, and his chances of defeating them were diminishing. Because of this, the enemy's plan elevated to a plot to cause confusion and kill them to stop the work. Nehemiah once again stood in prayer and set protection around them day and night. It is so crucial to point out that Nehemiah had a **strong prayer life** and connection with the Lord and his prayers were not idle. They always led him into action and brought him divine strategy, guidance, and instruction from heaven. Apostolic governors are strong prayer warriors with a consistent life of prayer. They are those who are led into action by prayer.

Nehemiah set a guard of protection around them day and night and he positioned them with their weapons in the openings that were left as they were completing the wall. He discerned that it was necessary for them to heighten their fortification for the safety of the people and the protection of the work. He discerned the times of when to fight and when to set protection. He was strategic in how he positioned them with their weapons. They could have been all over the city watching for the enemy with their weapons, and they could have kept working and had their weapons down beside them. But Nehemiah set them exactly where they needed to be in a strategic way that would fortify, protect, and cover them most efficiently against the enemy. He closed up all openings and left no room for the enemy to infiltrate and stop the work.

Apostolic governors discern the times and seasons of warfare. They know when to engage, and when to guard. They have a strategic blueprint for how to set up their soldiers and have a keen ability to detect the openings and fill them such that the enemy has no way in. They recognize when the warfare has heightened, and they increase the fortification accordingly so that the people and the work are covered. They take care of their people. They do not just tell the vision carriers that it is a time of intense warfare and leave them to figure out how to protect and engage in the warfare for themselves. They give them direction, guidance, and position them to cover themselves and the work fitly.

Nehemiah said to them, "Do not be afraid of them. Remember the Lord, who is great and awesome, and fight for your brothers, your sons, your daughters, your wives, and your homes." He kept them encouraged, focused, and empowered as they continued to go forward in the work. He made sure that their eyes were fixed on Jesus and who he was as their great and mighty God. As he told them to fight for their families and homes, he refreshed the vision and purpose of the assignment within them. It was like he gave them a heart shock and revived them.

As the warfare increases, apostolic governors will keep those who are vision carriers encouraged, empowered, and focused on the assignment. They do not allow them to be drawn away by discouragement, fear, depression, and distraction that comes due to intense bouts of warfare. They are those who carry a spirit of encouragement that uplifts, heals, and revives those building with them.

> ***Nehemiah 4:15-23 English Standard Version***
> *When our enemies heard that it was known to us and that God had frustrated their plan, we all returned to the wall, each to his work. From that day on, half of my servants worked on construction, and half held the spears, shields, bows, and coats of mail. And the leaders stood behind the whole house of Judah, who were building on the wall. Those who carried burdens were loaded in such a way that each*

labored on the work with one hand and held his weapon with the other. And each of the builders had his sword strapped at his side while he built. The man who sounded the trumpet was beside me. And I said to the nobles and to the officials and to the rest of the people, "The work is great and widely spread, and we are separated on the wall, far from one another. In the place where you hear the sound of the trumpet, rally to us there. Our God will fight for us."

So we labored at the work, and half of them held the spears from the break of dawn until the stars came out. I also said to the people at that time, "Let every man and his servant pass the night within Jerusalem, that they may be a guard for us by night and may labor by day." So neither I nor my brothers nor my servants nor the men of the guard who followed me, none of us took off our clothes; each kept his weapon at his right hand.

And I said unto the nobles, and to the rulers, and to the rest of the people, The work is great and large, and we are separated upon the wall, one far from another. In what place therefore ye hear the sound of the trumpet, resort ye thither unto us: our God shall fight for us. So we laboured in the work: and half of them held the spears from the rising of the morning till the stars appeared. Likewise at the same time said I unto the people, Let every one with his servant lodge within Jerusalem, that in the night they may be a guard to us, and labour on the day. So neither I, nor my brethren, nor my servants, nor the men of the guard which followed me, none of us put off our clothes, saving that every one put them off for washing.

The workers returned to the wall to continue with their work because Nehemiah frustrated the enemy's plans. Some worked while simultaneously holding their weapons, while others stood behind them protecting them. They worked with one hand while holding their weapon in the other. They knew how to multitask, and were aware of the importance of working and protecting the work at the same time. Often we get so zoned in and focused on the work that we forget to protect it. Time after time the work takes hits, never being fully built and completed. Nehemiah and his team knew how to work and guard at the same time and they kept their weapons strapped to them.

Apostolic governors are multi-taskers. They know how to work and guard at the same time so that their work is never jeopardized or left unprotected. They are balanced and do not become so honed in on the work and assignment at hand that they forget about the sneakiness of the enemy. Their weapons stay ready at all times. They are experts at guarding what God places in their hands. As one who is a vision carrier, planter, founder, elder, armor-bearer and more, I have had to master the art of multi-tasking. God gave me multiple responsibilities quite early on in my destiny walk, and I believe this is because he wanted to teach and cultivate me in those areas through a high level of spiritual exposure. Some of the prominent keys I have gained are balance, healthy time management, consistency, accountability, personal responsibility, time for refreshing, cleansing and recharging, staying in the strength of God, and communication. You will not succeed in multi-tasking if these keys are not implemented as you juggle through the different responsibilities God places in your life. God sees your capacity and gives you tasks because he knows you can handle them and flourish. However, you cannot do it alone in your own strength. You must rely on God and know that as you govern every area efficiently, you are like a weapon guarding over those aspects of your life and those impacted by the fulfillment of your responsibilities.

Nehemiah 5:1-6 And there was a great cry of the people and of their wives against their brethren the Jews. For there were that said, We, our sons, and our daughters, are many: therefore we take up corn for them, that we may eat, and live. Some also there were that said, We have mortgaged our lands, vineyards, and houses, that we might buy corn, because of the dearth. There were also that said, We have borrowed money for the king's tribute, and that upon our lands and vineyards. Yet now our flesh is as the flesh of our brethren, our children as their children: and, lo, we bring into bondage our sons and our daughters to be servants, and some of our daughters are brought unto bondage already: neither is it in our power to redeem them; for other men have our lands and vineyards. And I was very angry when I heard their cry and these words.

The people rose into a great cry because the demands of excessive taxing had caused distress to their lives. Many of the people had lost their land because of the excessive taxing, and some had their children taken into slavery. When Nehemiah heard of the condition of the people, his response was anger.

In our modern world, anger is considered a negative emotion; however, in the role of a gatekeeper (spiritually), anger becomes an energy that inspires action. Those of us who are called to the role of apostolic governor will see through the natural environment of a situation (the people's poverty) and interpret it through spiritual eyes. Anger is a legitimate force.

Question for consideration, "Have you ever found yourself angry and did not know what to do with why you were feeling that way?"

Do not think it is strange when you become angry, because it is part of your spiritual DNA. As apostolic governors, we have the heart of God, a passion for God's people, and a burden for the assignments given to us. The hurts, wounds, and oppression of God's people will cause us to be fired up! Let your anger blaze to bring about change and produce kingdom results! Be angry and sin not (Ephesians 4:26).

What is the last situation that you faced that provoked you to anger?

How could you have changed your response to the situation?

Learn to use your anger as fuel for the courage to confront situations and face challenges directly.

The bondage they were experiencing were the workings of a demonic principality of oppression, poverty, and slavery that was reigning over their region. So, Nehemiah, the gatekeeper was set into action.

> ***Nehemiah 5:7-11*** *I took counsel with myself, and I brought charges against the nobles and the officials. I said to them, "You are exacting interest, each from his brother." And I held a great assembly against them and said to them, "We, as far as we are able, have bought back our Jewish brothers who have been sold to the nations, but you even sell your brothers that they may be sold to us!" They were silent and could not find a word to say. So I said, "The thing that you are doing is not good. Ought you not to walk in the fear of our God to prevent the taunts of the nations our enemies? Moreover, I and my brothers and my servants are lending them money and grain. Let us abandon this exacting of interest. Return to them this very day their fields, their vineyards, their olive orchards, and their houses, and the percentage of money, grain, wine, and oil that you have been exacting from them."*

Nehemiah brought charges against the nobles and officials, told them of their wrongdoings and commanded them to restore to the Jewish brothers their possessions.

<u>*Rebuke*</u> in the Strong's in this scripture means:

1. To strive, contend
2. To strive; physically; with words
3. To conduct a case or suit (legal), sue
4. To make complaint
5. To quarrel

6. To contend against

Nehemiah contended against and quarreled with the enemy. He brought a legal case before a congregation and sued the demonic principalities for all that they had stolen. Apostolic governors are not afraid of confrontation and contention with the enemy. They are not scared to tell the enemy to give them back what he stole and take claim of it.

> ***Nehemiah 5:12-13*** *Then said they, We will restore them, and will require nothing of them; so will we do as thou sayest. Then I called the priests, and took an oath of them, that they should do according to this promise. Also I shook my lap, and said, So God shake out every man from his house, and from his labour, that performeth not this promise, even thus be he shaken out, and emptied. And all the congregation said, Amen, and praised the Lord. And the people did according to this promise.*

After Nehemiah confronted the enemy, they surrendered and said that they would return the possessions of the people and require nothing further from them. The people of Jerusalem obtained full freedom and were legally liberated from the bondage of oppression and poverty. Nehemiah then shook his lap.

<u>*Shook* in the Strong's in this scripture means:</u>

1. Overthrow
2. Toss up and down
3. To shake out or off
4. Show emptiness

5. To shake oneself

As he shook his lap he was overthrowing, tossing up and down, and emptying himself of the situation. This was symbolic of the full release of the judgment on the enemy's head. It was him relinquishing the matter from his hands such that he was no longer carrying the burden of the judgment within himself. He said "So may God shake out every man from his house and from his labor who does not keep this promise. So may he be shaken out and emptied." It was a prophetic act of what would happen if they did not follow through with the oath that they had made. The scripture confirms that the nobles and officials did follow through with all that they promised.

Apostolic governors know when to relinquish and empty themselves of the judgments they release toward the enemy. They know how take matters out of their hands and let the fullness of the judgment go forth. They are in tune with the prophetic spirit and movement of the Lord, and they will carry out prophetic acts of judgment and declaration that will seal the deal of the case.

Part 1
Reflection Questions

1. How do you handle your challenges? Are you overcome with your emotions to the point where you have no ability to seek God for solutions to the problem? In what ways can you grow in being a solutions seeker?

2. What has God led you to do that you know you need to receive his strategic plans for before you can go forward? Spend time praying about this and asking God to fill you with the strategy and plans that you need to begin in this season. Journal what he says and write out the steps in depth. Set a date for beginning to implement the plan.

3. What ways have/or is the enemy trying to come against who you are and what you have been called to do? After you list your points, write a one or two sentence decree to build yourself up against the attack and fill yourself with truth. For example if you have been battling sickness you can write something like I decree I am healed and whole because God said that by his stripes I am healed and that no weapon formed against me will prosper. I decree every weapon of sickness is no longer prospering in me.

4. In what ways can you grow in your prayer life and become more skilled in utilizing prayer strategies?

5. It takes multi-tasking abilities to be able to go forward in the work while simultaneously protecting it. How can you grow as a multi-tasker?

6. What things anger and stir you in society and the world today? Do you have a desire to bring forth change in those areas? Pray and ask God if these desires were placed there by him so that he could use you. Journal what he says and when you feel the urges stirring in you, seek God for what you are to do.

Part 2
Nehemiah: The Apostolic Governor

Nehemiah 5:14-15 English Standard Version
Moreover, from the time that I was appointed to be their governor in the land of Judah, from the twentieth year to the thirty-second year of Artaxerxes the king, twelve years, neither I nor my brothers ate the food allowance of the governor. The former governors who were before me laid heavy burdens on the people and took from them for their daily ration forty shekels of silver. Even their servants lorded it over the people. But I did not do so, because of the fear of God.

Nehemiah was appointed as the governor over the land of Judah, but he did not engage in the customary practices of the governor. The governors before him placed their own charges on the people and had personal food and wine portions. However, Nehemiah had his own vision and design as an apostolic governor and went forth in his unique identity and calling. He governed in a way that was pleasing to God and was fueled to do right by the people and the land because of the fear of the Lord. He knew that the fear of the Lord was the beginning of wisdom and that good understanding would follow (Psalm 111:10).

> **Psalms 111:10** *The fear of the Lord is the beginning of wisdom: a good understanding have all they that do his commandments: his praise endureth for ever.*

Apostolic governors have their own unique blueprint in the earth and will not lead the same as others. They do not take from what is familiar and normal and make it their own. They take what is from heaven's design in them, enmesh with it, and function from this place. Apostolic governors are okay with the fact that there is no one on this earth that will operate like them completely. They may see measures of themselves in other people and they will be able to learn and receive from them. Yet, all that they learn and receive will filter through God's unique identity and calling that is upon them. Apostolic governors are the first of their kind. They recognize the previous abuse of the people and land that they govern and they do not continue in that fashion. They function in new ways and establish new systems that are led by the Lord. As a result, they bring forth healing and restoration to the people and land. Through my destiny journey I have learned that no matter how many great teaching videos I watch, equipping books I read, conferences I attend, sermons I listen too, I will never find anyone who is just like me. I would be frustrated by this because it would make me feel alone, like I did not fit in, and that I was doing things wrong because it was different. At times, I would feel an inner discomfort because I did not understand why I had certain feelings toward ministry, how to run my company, purity, standards, righteousness, living a completely sold out life in Jesus because these things were not being broadcast as attributes to be desired. Some of the unique qualities gave me are I am a selfless servant leader, a leader of leaders, carrier of grace and raw power, a giant slayer and although I knew people who walked in measures of each of these, there was no one who walked in all of these. Seeing someone who is just like you can make you feel more comfortable about who you are, but taking on the attributes of another person that you did not spend the time, do the work, or pay the cost for results in the forfeiture of your unique journey and self-discovery process. The authenticity of God's image in you will be aborted and never effect those who God wanted it to. This is why it is crucially important to know that we are our own unique blueprint in the earth and God is the one who will build us in that. As I began to live by this, I found peace in being my own blueprint. Knowing that there was only one me and that God made me in a specific design brought me joy and motivated me to discover who that person was. It is easy to identify with another human being because you can constantly see them. You can make comparisons between you and them while seeing qualities you believe you embody within yourself. It is okay to receive impartation, to be elevated by others, and see remnants of yourself in people you admire. However, we were made in the image of God and only the creator (God) can reveal to us the FULLNESS of our image and identity. When I began to live by this, the Holy Spirit was able to speak to me about my unique identity distinctions. At times, my journal pages for certain months would be filled with insight on why I was the way I was and how it would be used for his glory. I was led to begin a declaration of who I am in the Lord in my journal in 2014. God instructed me to write down what he speaks to me about my identity each time something new was revealed. What began as 10 points in 2014, has evolved currently into 67 points of who God has said I am. Some of them have come into manifestation, while others are birthing in me for the future. When you find peace in being the only you, the one who created you will show you, YOU.

> ***Nehemiah 5:16*** *I also persevered in the work on this wall, and we acquired no land, and all my servants were gathered there for the work.*

Even though Nehemiah was appointed governor over the land of Judah, he continued in the work of the wall. He did not allow his promotion to take his focus and shift his vision. No matter the increase, his assignment was still to build the wall and restore the city. He did not get prideful and haughty and say "Oh I am governor now, I am going to do other things while the people continue the building work." He did not let the seat of the governor become a high place. This promotion was only a natural manifestation and ordination of what had already occurred in the spirit realm because he was the established gatekeeper when he claimed jurisdiction over the land.

Apostolic governors must not allow the natural elevation to become a high place, but a godly platform to further catapult us deeper into the depths of destiny, and a means for our reach and influence to be expanded. Apostolic governors keep their eyes on the work and do not think of themselves more highly than they ought (Romans 12:3). They do not act as if they are better than the people who serve them or serve with them. They are down in the nitty gritty of the work with the vision carriers. They do not just carry the vision but they do the work that births out the vision. In their promotion, they achieve power and authority for effectively completing their assignment, both naturally and spiritually.

> ***Romans 12:3 English Standard Version*** *For by the grace given to me I say to everyone among you not to think of himself more highly than he ought to think, but to think with sober judgment, each according to the measure of faith that God has assigned.*

> ***Nehemiah 5:17-19 English Standard Version*** *Moreover, there were at my table 150 men, Jews and officials, besides those who came to us from the nations that were around us. Now what was prepared at my expense for each day was one ox and six choice sheep and birds, and every ten days all kinds of wine in abundance. Yet for all this I did not demand the food allowance of the governor, because the service was too heavy on this people. Remember for my good, O my God, all that I have done for this people.*

Nehemiah regularly had the people of the land, 150 people to eat from his table. This included Jews, officials, and those who came from other nations. He was like an apostolic ambassador. Can you imagine having that many people over your house eating from your table? Apostolic governors have to be okay with inviting people and strangers into their homes as God leads. They are the ambassadorial officials of their sphere of influence. Their tables and homes must be open and accessible to the people. The word table is symbolic of communion, fellowship, relationship, proximity. Apostolic governors need to have close fellowship and communion with the people that God entrusts to them. This helps to build relationship, and gives greater awareness of who and what is coming into the gates of their sphere. In strategic leadership, Nehemiah displayed cultural agility. His ability to entertain people from other nations meant that he interacted with people outside of his religious and social norms, and he could influence diverse groups of people.

Nehemiah did not take from the people the governors allowance because he knew that the burden was too heavy for them. All that he required of them was what he needed to give back to the people and accommodate those who ate from his table. He was sensitive to the needs and conditions of the people.

Apostolic governors are aware when things are too heavy and will adjust so that the assignment is supplied for but the people are also taken care of in the process of the work as well. At times, for leaders the work can become more important than the conditions of the people, but a healthy balance is essential. Apostolic governors know how to balance the needs of the assignment and the needs of those who are vision carriers serving and working with them. They do not mistreat their people. They have a heart and genuine love for them.

> ***Nehemiah 6:1-4*** *Now it came to pass, when Sanballat, and Tobiah, and Geshem the Arabian, and the rest of our enemies, heard that I had builded the wall, and that there was no breach left therein; (though at that time I had not set up the doors upon the gates;) That Sanballat and Geshem sent unto me, saying, Come, let us meet together in some one of the villages in the plain of Ono. But they thought to do me mischief. And I sent messengers unto them, saying, I am doing a great work, so that I cannot come down: why should the work cease, whilst I leave it, and come down to you?*

Sanballat, Tobiah, and Geshem got word that the wall was built and that there were no longer any breaches left. However, the doors on the gates had not been set so they found their way in to try to hinder the final part of the work. No matter how close we get to finishing the assignment, we cannot let our guard up and become lax in our discernment to detect the work of the enemy. It was important for Nehemiah to stay fortified and sharp because even though the wall was built, the doors had not yet been set. Sanballat and Geshem sent to him saying "Come and let us meet together," but Nehemiah knew that they didn't just want to meet. Once again the enemy recognized that the work was getting closer to being done and he planned to kill Nehemiah. When your assignment is almost done the enemy will try to find a way to get close to you. Your eyes and your ears must be spiritually in tune to discern the hidden motives and the voice of the enemy so that you do not come into enemy territory.

Nehemiah then sent messengers to tell them that he could not come down from his work and that the work should not stop for him to meet with them.

<u>Down</u> in the Strong's in this scripture means:

1. To go down, descend, decline, march down, sink down
2. To go or come down
3. To sink
4. To be prostrated
5. To come down (of revelation)
6. To bring down
7. To send down
8. To take down
9. To lay prostrate
10. To let down
11. To be brought down
12. To be taken down

Had Nehemiah come down to meet with them he would have:

- Come down from the elevated place of revelation
- Surrendered to be brought and taken down by the enemy

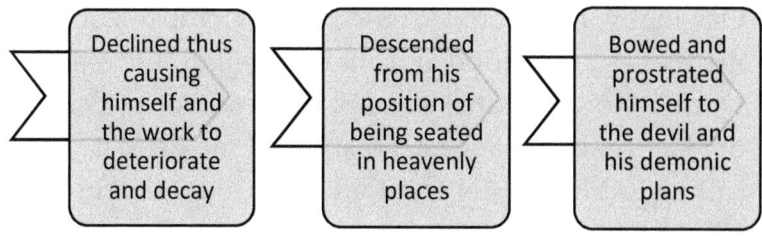

Apostolic governors must not come down from their ascended place with God. They must remain seated in heavenly places of revelation so that the work can continue and not be aborted. The elevation keeps them surrendered to God and the vision. They do not bow to the plans of the enemy, thus exposing themselves.

> *Nehemiah 6:4-9 English Standard Version And they sent to me four times in this way, and I answered them in the same manner. In the same way Sanballat for the fifth time sent his servant to me with an open letter in his hand. In it was written, "It is reported among the nations, and Geshem also says it, that you and the Jews intend to rebel; that is why you are building the wall. And according to these reports you wish to become their king. And you have also set up prophets to proclaim concerning you in Jerusalem, 'There is a king in Judah.' And now the king will hear of these reports. So now come and let us take counsel together." Then I sent to him, saying, "No such things as you say have been done, for you are inventing them out of your own mind." For they all wanted to frighten us, thinking, "Their hands will drop from the work, and it will not be done." But now, O God, strengthen my hands.*

Originally, I thought I would return home to get on my feet as I transitioned from college into the real world. However, this was not my testimony. During my last year of college, God showed me I had a calling to Muncie, IN and that I was to remain in the region to continue plowing kingdom work and cultivating my destiny. This was difficult for me and others to understand because it was out of the norm. Having such a drastic change in the vision plan for my life was tough for some and respectfully so. They had watched me grow up, supported me, sheltered me, nurtured me and on and on. I had a great support system and they were accustomed to me acting and responding a certain way. When God shifted my plans, it was challenging. It would have been better if I was relocating for the start of a great career, but I was following the guidance of Lord which many talk about, but do not actually live by in the daily decisions that shape their lives. I could not come down from the ascended place of destiny God set me in. He was shifting me and they now had to learn the new me, understand my changes, and embrace the vision God shifted me into. It was a shift for everybody, but I was the person receiving the revelation from God, while the others aiming to understand, needed time and grace to come into this. Vigorous prayer, the encouragement of those who saw my calling, and books on aligning with destiny carried me through this season. This was not to defend myself, but to help me stand and continue with God despite the challenges and questions of others. It kept me uplifted during bouts of sadness and discouragement due to feeling lonely, rejected and misunderstood. As I read the books on destiny and received prayer, I understood that this was all a part of the journey and that my trials were a part of my stance in God. Although it was a hard decision, the fruit of it has blossomed excellently in my life. Stay with God and he will allow the fruit to be your testimony.

Four different times they asked Nehemiah to come down from the work and each time he gave them the same response. The enemy was persistent, but so was Nehemiah. We must relentlessly stand in the Lord and the assignment no matter how many times the enemy tries to get us to come down. Our response must remain the same, "No devil! We will not come down and stop the work." Apostolic governors are those who are disciplined in consistency.

The fourth time the devil realized that his plan was not working, so the fifth time he tried something a bit different. If he could not get Nehemiah to come down to meet with them, he planned to give him a reason to come down by lying on him, slandering the work, his character and reputation as a leader. This is representation that the enemy has now become desperate in his plans. He chooses to lie on you to discredit the work and your identity. He sends a personal attack of defamation of character designed to hit you closer to home and falter you.

Sanballat, Tobiah, and Geshem presented the false allegations to him and then said, "Come now therefore, and let us take counsel together."

Counsel in the Strong's means:

1. To say, speak, utter
2. To say, to answer, to say in one's heart, to think, to command, to promise, to intend
3. To be told, to be said, to be called
4. To boast, act proudly
5. To avow, to avouch

Had Nehemiah come down to take counsel with them he would have been forming a demonic covenant, making demonic promises, and taking demonic vows. Apostolic governors do NOT have conversations with the devil, and we surely do not make deals with him! Nehemiah recognized the lie, called the bluff, and spoke the truth to set the record straight. He called them out and exposed that they created the allegations from their own mind and heart. They were releasing fantasy and he was not drawn into an unnecessary fight of trying to clear his good name since he knew that it was not reality. When the enemy releases falsehoods against apostolic governors, they do not fight wars of fantasy and false reality. They remain positioned within reality and handle things from that place. Apostolic governors do not give the enemy the satisfaction of reacting to his petty lies. They continue the assignment persisting in truth.

Nehemiah recognized the plan of the enemy was to frighten and distract them to stop the work. He said, "For they all wanted to frighten us, thinking, "Their hands will drop from the work, and it will not be done." But now, O God, strengthen my hands."

Strengthen in the Strong's in this scripture means:

1. To strengthen, prevail, harden, be strong, become strong, be courageous, be firm, grow firm, be resolute, be sore
2. To prevail, to be firm, be caught fast, secure
3. To press, be urgent
4. To grow stout, grow hard
5. To restore to strength, give strength
6. To strengthen, sustain, encourage
7. To make strong, make bold
8. To make firm, to make rigid, make strong
9. To repair
10. To withstand

Nehemiah prayed to the Lord for increased strength to finish the work. Since the warfare was increasing, he acknowledged that it was time to refresh and restore from the warfare drainages he endured through the process. The secret plans of the enemy were to weaken them to stop the work, so Nehemiah's prayer for strength was a **counteractive prayer** to combat the demonic curses that were being released. He received strength, courage, and empowerment to become further established to carry on the work. It was like he enmeshed with his assignment deeper, and was hardened like an immovable statue- set like flint to complete the task.

> **Isaiah 50:7** *For the Lord God will help me; therefore shall I not be confounded: therefore have I set my face like a flint,*

Apostolic governors know how to pray prayers that will counterattack the enemy. They are keen in their ability to discern and bring exposure to the secret motives of the enemy that are purposed for their destruction. Due to bouts of warfare that may seem to be a lot during intense building and establishing, they know when it is time to pray and ask the Lord to refresh, encourage, and help them press in the work. They become the literal embodiment of the work, being made like statues and flint, firmly stout, rigid and resolute within it.

> *Nehemiah 6:10-14 English Standard Version*
> *Now when I went into the house of Shemaiah the son of Delaiah, son of Mehetabel, who was confined to his home, he said, "Let us meet together in the house of God, within the temple. Let us close the doors of the temple, for they are coming to kill you. They are coming to kill you by night." But I said, "Should such a man as I run away? And what man such as I could go into the temple and live? I will not go in." And I understood and saw that God had not sent him, but he had pronounced the prophecy against me because Tobiah and Sanballat had hired him. For this purpose he was hired, that I should be afraid and act in this way and sin, and so they could give me a bad name in order to taunt me. Remember Tobiah and Sanballat, O my God, according to these things that they did, and also the prophetess Noadiah and the rest of the prophets who wanted to make me afraid.*

Shemaiah asked Nehemiah to meet with him in the house of God within the temple because Tobiah and Sanballat were coming to kill him. Nehemiah's immediate response is, "Should such a man as I run away? And what man such as I could go into the temple and live?" He was not scared of facing death and was devoted to staying in the work despite the danger. Apostolic governors do not run from the enemy and the challenges that arise with walking in their calling and fulfilling their assignments. They are devoted and loyal no matter the cost. He said why should I go into the temple (which should be a place of shelter and covering) and live. He was sold out to his assignment and preferred to work and face death rather than to come down for shelter while the city and his people perished. He perceived the truth and his spiritual senses were keen to see the "house of God" for the trap that it was. Shemaiah had not been sent by God and was on assignment to instill fear, cause him to sin by coming out of alignment with God, and slander his name. He was a demonic agent who had been hired to pronounce false prophecy over him to trick him. Shemaiah used witchcraft to entice Nehemiah by using the house of God. Nehemiah should have been able to trust this man as he was supposed to be a part of the house of God, but truly he was false prophet using witchcraft tactics.

Apostolic governors are keen in discerning witchcraft and are on guard against it no matter who the person is. The enemy will go to all kinds of lengths and depths to trap us and thwart the fulfillment of our assignment. He will use the church itself, those in the church, friends, family, and loved ones. The devil does not care, so we must try every spirit. We should be quick to listen and hear from the Lord such that we can discern demonic agents from Gods agents, a true prophecy from a false prophecy, and when the devil is using someone against us who would normally be seen as good and beneficial to our lives.

> ***Matthew 7:15*** *Beware of false prophets, which come to you in sheep's clothing, but inwardly they are ravening wolves.*

> ***1 John 4:1*** *Beloved, believe not every spirit, but try the spirits whether they are of God: because many false prophets are gone out into the world.*

If Nehemiah would have come down to the house of God it would have been representative of him being lured by a sense of false protection. Religion would have said that coming down to the house of God would protect him from being killed as he would be closer to God, but his true relationship and connection with God revealed to him that this was not true. God was with Nehemiah and his hand of goodness and favor was upon him. God was internally with him as he had a devoted consistent prayer life and walked in close communion with the Lord to be guided and strengthened by him. The enemy wanted to pull him from that fortified place to the false representation of protection he presented by telling him to meet him in the house of God. The house of God was merely a building, but Nehemiah's relationship with the Lord was highly fortified and impenetrable to the enemy. That was true protection. We cannot be swayed by feeding into religion rather than the truth of our established relationship and connection with the Lord. Do not be fooled by the religious, stay in the spirit with God.

Nehemiah goes on to say, "Remember Tobiah and Sanballat, O my God, according to these things that they did, and also the prophetess Noahdiah and the rest of the prophets who wanted to make me afraid."

Wow! There was a host of false prophets operating against Nehemiah and the people of Jerusalem finishing the wall and restoring the city, but this did not distress him. He remained positioned as the gatekeeper, judge, and governor of his region, and once again released judgment onto the heads of the false prophets. Apostolic governors remain seated as judges so that they can consistently judge the enemy as necessary.

> ***Nehemiah 6:15-19 English Standard Version*** *So the wall was finished on the twenty-fifth day of the month Elul, in fifty-two days. And when all our enemies heard of it, all the nations around us were afraid and fell greatly in their own esteem, for they perceived that this work had been accomplished with the help of our God. Moreover, in those days the nobles of Judah sent many letters to Tobiah, and Tobiah's letters came to them. For many in Judah were bound by oath to him, because he was the son-in-law of Shecaniah the son of Arah: and his son Jehohanan had taken the daughter of Meshullam the son of Berechiah as his wife. Also they spoke of his good deeds in my presence and reported my words to him. And Tobiah sent letters to make me afraid.*

The wall was now complete and when their enemies got word of this they were afraid and low in their esteem because they knew that God had been with

Nehemiah and the workers. They were intimidated, so to find a way to break through the fortified wall, Tobiah sent letters to Nehemiah as a fear tactic. Isn't it interesting that Nehemiah's authority was initially validated by letters from King Artaxerxes, and now Tobiah is attempting to use letters to discredit him? The devil is a copycat at best. He has no originality in his schemes. The most he can hope to do is illegitimately mimic something that is legitimate in your life. After you complete a portion of your assignment the enemy will try to find ways to sift it to eventually knock it down. As apostolic governors, we must continue to be fearless and fortified even after the work is completed such that we give no room for the devil to gain a foothold. There are times where we establish a great work and fall into the fear traps of the enemy that poke holes in what we have built, thus creating an open door for the enemy to infiltrate. Be mindful of these traps such that we do not put in jeopardy what we have worked so diligently to build.

> ***Nehemiah 7:1-4 English Standard Version*** *Now when the wall had been built and I had set up the doors, and the gatekeepers, the singers, and the Levites had been appointed, I gave my brother Hanani and Hananiah the governor of the castle charge over Jerusalem, for he was a more faithful and God-fearing man than many. And I said to them, "Let not the gates of Jerusalem be opened until the sun is hot. And while they are still standing guard, let them shut and bar the doors. Appoint guards from among the inhabitants of Jerusalem, some at their guard posts and some in*

> *front of their own homes." The city was wide and large, but the people within it were few, and no houses had been rebuilt.*

The wall was built and Nehemiah went forth in appointing gatekeepers, singers, and Levites, and gave his brother Hanani, and Hananiah who was governor over the castle charge over Jerusalem. He set instruction on how to govern the gate and appointed people to the guard post and in front of their homes as well. He was delegating responsibility to those who could be trusted and whose character was in proper condition to continue the work as he said, "For he was a more faithful and God-fearing man than many." Nehemiah said that the city was large, there were not many people living there, and no houses had been rebuilt. The fullness of the restoration inside of the city had not yet been completed which made it critical that the right people be appointed as leaders because the work was still fragile.

> **Nehemiah 7:5** *And my God put into mine heart to gather together the nobles, and the rulers, and the people, that they might be reckoned by genealogy. And I found a register of the genealogy of them which came up at the first, and found written therein,*

Since there were not many people living there and the city needed to be fully restored, God placed it in Nehemiah's heart to register the people. Nehemiah was restoring the generations, documenting, and legalizing the exiled people of Jerusalem.

Register in the Strong's in this scripture means:

1. Properly writing, a book, bill, evidence, letter
2. Missive, document
3. Letter (of instruction), written order, commission, request, written decree
4. Legal document, certificate of divorce, deed of purchase, indictment, sign
5. Book, scroll
6. Book of prophecies
7. Genealogical register
8. Law book
9. Record book (of God)

Nehemiah was recording the names of the returned people in the record book of God. He was documenting their legal divorce from bondage and their deed of purchase by God as his chosen people. He was creating a missive which is a written message and letter from an official source, further hedging and closing them in protection as God's people. He was restoring them in covenant with God as he identified and provided evidence that they belonged to God. He was yet closing another breach and opening for the enemy by restoring the generations in covenant with the Lord.

Apostolic governors are generationally-minded and have heart to restore the generations such that the covenant of God will be multiplied from generation to generation. Their eyes are wide open to see the entirety of the assignment so they can detect the openings that the enemy can potentially use. They receive divine ideas and strategies from the Lord on how to fortify efficiently and further plow the work. Nehemiah not only closed a breach but he restored a lost and exiled people to their God.

> ***Nehemiah 8:1-3*** *And all the people gathered themselves together as one man into the street that was before the water gate; and they spake unto Ezra the scribe to bring the book of the law of Moses, which the Lord had commanded to Israel. And Ezra the priest brought the law before the congregation both of men and women, and all that could hear with understanding, upon the first day of the seventh month. And he read therein before the street that was before the water gate from the morning until midday, before the men and the women, and those that could understand; and the ears of all the people were attentive unto the book of the law.*

> ***Nehemiah 8:13-15*** *And on the second day were gathered together the chief of the fathers of all the people, the priests, and the Levites, unto Ezra the scribe, even to understand the words of the law. And they found written in the law which the Lord had commanded by Moses, that the children of Israel should dwell in booths in the feast of the seventh month: And that they should publish and proclaim in all their cities, and in Jerusalem, saying, Go forth unto the mount, and fetch olive branches, and pine branches, and myrtle branches, and palm branches, and branches of thick trees, to make booths, as it is written.*

> ***Nehemiah 8:18*** *Also day by day, from the first day unto the last day, he read in the book of the law of God. And they kept the feast seven days; and on the*

eighth day was a solemn assembly, according unto the manner.

Nehemiah 12:27-30 *And at the dedication of the wall of Jerusalem they sought the Levites out of all their places, to bring them to Jerusalem, to keep the dedication with gladness, both with thanksgivings, and with singing, with cymbals, psalteries, and with harps. And the sons of the singers gathered themselves together, both out of the plain country round about Jerusalem, and from the villages of Netophathi; Also from the house of Gilgal, and out of the fields of Geba and Azmaveth: for the singers had builded them villages round about Jerusalem. And the priests and the Levites purified themselves, and purified the people, and the gates, and the wall.*

The people gathered together as one in the city to partake of the reading of the book of the Law of Moses by Ezra the priest. The people of the city were united which displayed the fruit of their restored covenant. They stood before the priest to go even deeper in covenant by receiving the establishing of the commandments of the Lord. It was important to their restoration to receive teaching to shift them into following and living by the principles of the Lord. The people needed to be equipped in their ability to be obedient and walk in relationship with the Lord for themselves.

Nehemiah's apostolic character is strongly displayed as he builds and restores the people:

- He was sent to this region by God

- He claimed it back from the enemy by treading on the territory
- He judged the demonic principalities and powers of the air
- He rebuilt the land and fortified it
- He set people in position to govern over the land
- He restored the generations and covenant relationship with the Lord
- The people were taught the commandments and principles of the Lord
- He changed the whole atmosphere of this region and made the entire culture of the land and people to look like that of the one who sent him

Apostolic governors are those who teach and equip people to follow the commandments of the Lord so they can walk daily submitted lives. As they help people to be restored in relationship with God, they impart his standards and principles to them such that they can flourish personally with the Lord.

> ***Nehemiah 13:4-9 English Standard Version***
> *Now before this, Eliashib the priest, who was appointed over the chambers of the house of our God, and who was related to Tobiah, prepared for Tobiah a large chamber where they had previously put the grain offering, the frankincense, the vessels, and the tithes of grain, wine, and oil, which were given by commandment to the Levites, singers, and*

gatekeepers, and the contributions for the priests. While this was taking place, I was not in Jerusalem, for in the thirty-second year of Artaxerxes king of Babylon I went to the king. And after some time I asked leave of the king and came to Jerusalem, and I then discovered the evil that Eliashib had done for Tobiah, preparing for him a chamber in the courts of the house of God. And I was very angry, and I threw all the household furniture of Tobiah out of the chamber. Then I gave orders, and they cleansed the chambers, and I brought back there the vessels of the house of God, with the grain offering and the frankincense.

Eliashib the priest created a breach in the city by giving Tobiah place in the house of the Lord, and the Levites and singers were being robbed of their portions. Nehemiah was not present at the time of Eliashib's breach but came back into the region and brought correction. He set order amongst the treasurers, priests, and Levites such that they each received their portion. He had this authority because it was his sphere of influence and he was still operating as the apostolic governor over his assignment. Apostolic governors should be aligned with their entire sphere of influence such that we can detect breaches and set order accordingly.

> ***Matthew 21:12-13*** *And Jesus went into the temple of God, and cast out all them that sold and bought in the temple, and overthrew the tables of the moneychangers, and the seats of them that sold doves, And said unto them, It is written, My house*

shall be called the house of prayer; but ye have made it a den of thieves.

Nehemiah 13:15-22 *In those days I saw in Judah people treading winepresses on the Sabbath, and bringing in heaps of grain and loading them on donkeys, and also wine, grapes, figs, and all kinds of loads, which they brought into Jerusalem on the Sabbath day. And I warned them on the day when they sold food. Tyrians also, who lived in the city, brought in fish and all kinds of goods and sold them on the Sabbath to the people of Judah, in Jerusalem itself! Then I confronted the nobles of Judah and said to them, "What is this evil thing that you are doing, profaning the Sabbath day? Did not your fathers act in this way, and did not our God bring all this disaster on us and on this city? Now you are bringing more wrath on Israel by profaning the Sabbath."*

As soon as it began to grow dark at the gates of Jerusalem before the Sabbath, I commanded that the doors should be shut and gave orders that they should not be opened until after the Sabbath. And I stationed some of my servants at the gates, that no load might be brought in on the Sabbath day. Then the merchants and sellers of all kinds of wares lodged outside Jerusalem once or twice. But I warned them and said to them, "Why do you lodge outside the wall? If you do so again, I will lay hands on you." From that time on they did not come on the Sabbath. Then I commanded the Levites that they should purify themselves and come and guard the gates, to keep the Sabbath day holy. Remember

> *this also in my favor, O my God, and spare me according to the greatness of your steadfast love.*

The people were making sales on the Sabbath which was a sacred day concerning the commandments of the Lord. Nehemiah confronted the people to remind them that disobedience originally caused the disaster to come upon their city in the first place. Apostolic governors will keep their region and people in alignment such that they remember the directions of the Lord. They will bring correction and rebuke such that the region and city do not fall into continual disobedience and rebellion. He commanded that the gates be closed on the Sabbath and then opened after the Sabbath such that no sales and exchanges were taking place during the sacred time. As a gatekeeper, he orchestrated the gates of his region in accordance with the instruction of the Lord. When the gates were closed, the merchants would hang out on the outside of the gate. He warned them and said, "Why do you lodge outside the wall? If you do so again, I will lay hands on you." The *New Living Translation* of this scripture says, "What are you doing out here, camping around the wall? If you do this again, I will arrest you!" Apostolic governors arrest the enemy. They do not allow the enemy to just hang around their region even if he is outside of the gate. They know that the devil hangs out nearby to wait for his chance to infiltrate and draw people away so they take no chances.

Nehemiah continually towered over the enemy and thwarted attack after attack that came to hinder the work. From his journey, we receive the keys of strong skilled discernment, strategic prayer weapons, unique leadership abilities that empower and encourage, fearlessness and boldness against demonic oppositions and confrontations, and complete perseverance in fulfilling the assignments of the Lord. These keys will aid us as apostolic governors overcoming the demonic challenges we face as we journey to complete our destiny assignments.

Prayer:

Decreeing that even now the fierce, quick, keen, sharp, discerning anointing of Nehemiah fills you. That even as he was quick and sharp in his ability to extinguish the attacks of the enemy against his assignment and life that you would operate at this same magnitude and fierceness. Decreeing that you are being filled with perseverance and fortitude to pray continually and build a close communion relationship with the Lord that it would be easy to hear his voice and decipher his voice from the voice of the enemies and those who are set as a hindrance and resistance to your calling and what God grants to hands. Decreeing that as you become keen and sensitive to Gods voice that he will be able to give you direction and guidance in all that concerns you and you will be able to complete every assignment and govern over it continually such that it last eternally and those who are vision carriers of what God has granted to your hands will be able to sustain it, maintain it, and carry it even further. In Jesus name, it is so!

Part 2
Reflection Questions

1. What is your unique blueprint and identity? Although you may see measures of yourself in others, what is uniquely you that makes you the first of your kind?

2. Are there areas in your character that may try to hinder your growth in your calling? Fall out of agreement with those areas and journal them so that you can keep yourself accountable. Release them to the Lord so that he can cleanse you and process you to complete deliverance in these areas?

3. In what ways can you grow in communing and building relationship with those involved in your destiny journey?

4. How would you rate your discernment level on a scale from 1-10, 10 being the best? Why do you give that score? How can you improve this?

5. Write about a time you were persistent against the enemy and the challenges you were facing? What made you keep pressing forward? Write about a time you were not persistent? What caused you to stop pressing?

6. *How can you further embody your destiny and calling and become fixed like flint in it? Ask God to strengthen and harden you in who he has called you to be and what he has placed in your hands.*

7. *What fears, doubts, and worries do you have about your destiny and calling? Pray about these and ask God to cleanse them. They give the enemy an open door to hinder you.*

8. *In what ways can you be more aggressive and unapologetic when it comes to confronting the things of the enemy?*

Chapter 3
Mordecai & Esther: Apostolic Governing Covenant

The relationship of Mordecai and Esther shows one of an apostolic governing covenant. Mordecai counseled and protected Esther as she shifted from being his adopted daughter to the queen. Out of her elevation came his elevation and the deliverance of their people. Mordecai played a crucial role as Esther embarked on a new destiny shift journey, as without his apostolic governing it would not have been possible. We need these types of relationships because they make the fulfillment of our destiny and calling possible. They strengthen the fortifications of protection around our destiny and calling, and we are able to form strong close bonds with them as they care for us, sow into us, build us up, encourage us, guide and counsel us, lead us and shift us higher. We need the apostolic governing Mordecai's of our destiny!

> ***Esther 2:1-7*** *After these things, when the wrath of king Ahasuerus was appeased, he remembered Vashti, and what she had done, and what was decreed against her. Then said the king's servants that ministered unto him, Let there be fair young virgins sought for the king: And let the king appoint officers in all the provinces of his kingdom, that they may gather together all the fair young virgins unto Shushan the palace, to the house of the women, unto the custody of Hege the king's chamberlain, keeper of the women; and let their things for purification be given them: And let the maiden which pleaseth the king be queen instead of*

Vashti. And the thing pleased the king; and he did so. Now in Shushan the palace there was a certain Jew, whose name was Mordecai, the son of Jair, the son of Shimei, the son of Kish, a Benjamite; Who had been carried away from Jerusalem with the captivity which had been carried away with Jeconiah king of Judah, whom Nebuchadnezzar the king of Babylon had carried away. And he brought up Hadassah, that is, Esther, his uncle's daughter: for she had neither father nor mother, and the maid was fair and beautiful; whom Mordecai, when her father and mother were dead, took for his own daughter.

King Ahasuerus sent for all the fair young virgins such that he could select a new queen and Esther is one of those who is brought into the palace. The scripture says, "And he brought up Hadassah, that is, Esther, his uncle's daughter: for she had neither father nor mother, and the maid was fair and beautiful; whom Mordecai, when her father and mother were dead, took for his own daughter." After Esther's parents died, she was adopted and "brought up" by her cousin Mordecai.

<u>Brought up in the Strong's in this scripture means:</u>

1. To support, confirm, be faithful
2. Uphold, nourish,
3. Foster-father, foster-mother, nurse
4. Pillars, supporters of the door
5. To be established, be faithful, be carried, make firm
6. To be carried by a nurse, made firm, sure, lasting

7. Confirmed, established, sure, verified
8. Reliable, faithful, trusty
9. To stand firm, to be certain, to believe in

Mordecai was like Esther's spiritual father. He was a pillar and supporter of the doors of her life. They were in a faithful relationship with one another and he was her means of nourishment and validation. She was brought up in the nurture of these aspects, so their relationship had a strong foundation. In our lives, we need to be connected to our spiritual fathers and mothers or those who are assigned to our lives to help us govern our destiny and calling. If God has appointed them to that position, they are apostolic governors in our lives.

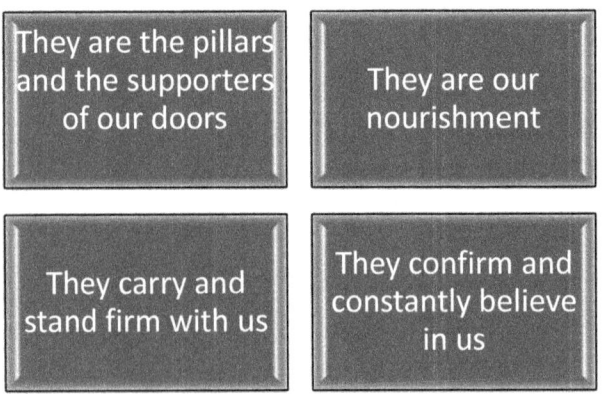

It is important to form spiritual relationships of reliability, and be raised in the four dynamics that are listed above. Out of this place of intimacy, destiny will flow, discipline will be molded, and structures of protection will be established.

> *Esther 2:10-11 Esther had not shewed her people nor her kindred:for Mordecai had charged her that she should not shew it. And Mordecai walked every day before the court of the women's house, to know how Esther did, and what should become of her.*

Mordecai directed Esther to conceal her nationality because had she told them who she was, it would have altered her chances of being chosen as queen. Additionally, it would have been detrimental during her reign as queen because of the political opposition against the Jews. Mordecai gave her sound and wise counsel to hide who she was until the time was right. Esther needed Mordecai's guidance because she was amid a transition, which at times can cause us to lose sight of important details. Mordecai had the ability to see from the outside looking in. He had a wider view to see what she could not see for herself. Spiritual mothers and fathers tend to have a better view of things because they can see the fullness of who we are before we do, thus, they can govern us and guide us to make the right decisions that can affect our destiny and calling.

Esther 2:11 says "And Mordecai walked **every day** before the court of the women's house, to know how Esther did, and what should become of her."

The key here is this type of governing relationship is an everyday kind of relationship, it is not:

- ✓ When we want it
- ✓ When we want advice and guidance
- ✓ When we want to give advice and guidance

- ✓ When it is a convenience
- ✓ When it is to just get us out of a stump
- ✓ When we are at church or doing ministry
- ✓ When we need something
- ✓ When we are lonely
- ✓ When we are zealous about our walk and destiny
- ✓ When we see others walking in their covenant
- ✓ When we want to show it off even though we do not value it
- ✓ When we feel comfortable, vulnerable, and open to it
- ✓ When we are having a good day and feel good
- ✓ When the conversation is good, but not when it is time for correction and constructive criticism
- ✓ When we are rested and are not tired, so we do not have to push and press
- ✓ When we are benefiting and profiting, but not when we have to give up things we value and sacrifice of ourselves

Mordecai's relationship with Esther was an everyday covenant. Daily he walked close to Esther's destiny so that he could be aware of her progress. He was invested in who she was, reliable as her support system, and trustworthy. It says he "walked every day."

Some of the meanings of *walked* in the Strong's in this scripture are:

1. Traveller
2. Journey

3. Traverse (which means he looked over, examined, reviewed, surveyed, and considered carefully what was going on with her as she was in the palace.)
4. Conversant (which means he remained familiar with the things that concerned her destiny because he studied it. He had regular conversation with her destiny as he walked every day before the court. He was intimately associated and acquainted with her destiny.)

Those we are in covenant with will diligently study all aspects of our destiny. They will want to know what is going and why so that they can pray, cover, and strengthen us as we go forward.

Esther 2:20 says, "Esther had not yet shewed her kindred nor her people; as Mordecai had charged her: for Esther did the commandment of Mordecai, like as when she was brought up with him." This was not Esther's first time being obedient and submissive to Mordecai's leadership. What they cultivated everyday was preparation for what they needed in the journey to greater destiny. Value of his guidance was an attribute of their relationship.

As we connect with covenant relationships that will help apostolically govern over our destiny and calling we must embody the attributes of:

Respect	Honor	Value	Submission

Obedience

We should practice these attributes until they are engrained into the foundation of our relationships and our nature. As God places us into the care of our spiritual mothers and fathers or leaders, they are accountable to God concerning us. We should honor their willingness, heart, and work they put into caring for us because they are keeping watch over OUR souls. We will benefit from who they are and what they do for our lives.

> ***Hebrews 13:17*** *Obey them that have the rule over you, and submit yourselves: for they watch for your souls, as they that must give account, that they may do it with joy, and not with grief: for that is unprofitable for you.*

Watch in this scripture means to be sleepless, keep awake, watch, to be circumspect, attentive, and ready (Strong's Concordance). They are operating from their position prudently, carefully, discreetly and observantly. They are laboring for us, with us, and even losing sleep to make sure that they take care of us so they can give a pleasing account to God concerning us. They should be blessed and joyous holding this office in our lives because it is "unprofitable" meaning of no benefit to us if they do their job with grief and not from a good and pure place. They should freely be able to exercise the fullness of their God-ordained authority to watch over us and give us direction.

As we submit to the governing leaders of our lives they make ready the paths of destiny for us. As Mordecai encouraged Esther, essentially, he had foreseen things to come and had already gone before her. With his covering, he was preparing the way for her. It is a key of apostolic governing to be connected to the people God has ordained for our lives to go before us and that have the influence and authority to walk us where they have already been.

Esther 2:17-19 And when the virgins were gathered together the second time, then Mordecai sat in the king's gate.

As Esther was established as queen, Mordecai was established at the king's gate. As she was destiny stationed, Mordecai was too. He positioned himself at the gate of her destiny.

<u>Sat</u> in the Strong's for this scripture means:

1. To abide
2. Dwell
3. To be inhabited
4. To sit down (specifically as judge in ambush, in quiet)
5. Establish
6. To remain
7. To marry- He was married to the vision

Mordecai's dwelling place became the destiny site of Esther. He was so deeply devoted to apostolically governing her life that he was married to it. The apostolic governors over our lives will conjoin with our destiny in this likeness. They will be there when the enemy attacks, and sit as a judge in ambush concerning our destiny and calling. We may have relationships with people who pray for us and share encouragement with us, but those who are appointed to have apostolic rule within our lives will form covenant with us that becomes their abiding place. They will marry the vision of God for our lives and commit to do life with us as we walk through destiny.

The Mordecai of my life is my spiritual mother. One day in church, God led me to go to the empty space in the back of the church and dance. At this time in my life, dance had become more of a discouragement because I began to have back problems and persistent body aches that made some movements difficult. I had changed my major from dance to exercise science because of the back problems and had resorted that any career I would have in dance was over. Even though I had trained in dance from my youth, I did not know it was a divine ministry gift and that God was going to use it for his glory in the near future. As I danced, it seemed as though the peace and refreshing waters of God flowed through my body as I freely worshipped him. I did not pay attention to anything and anyone around me as I was enraptured into a secret heavenly place with the Lord. That day was the beginning of a new adventure in dance. After the church service ended, a lady walked up to me and asked "Have you ever seen yourself dance before the Lord?" I shyly responded with a head nod no, and she proceeded to show me a video she shot of me dancing during the service. I watched in awe as I viewed this new expression I had never experienced before. She was the leader of the dance ministry of the church and became my mentor. She began to invite me to conferences to learn and cultivate my ministry of dance. We would spend time together praying, dancing, choreographing dances, discussing ministry, hanging out and as I watched her life, I learned about what it looked like to live solely for the Lord to fulfill your destiny and calling. As we built relationship, God revealed that she was my spiritual mother. She would nurture me in my calling, destiny and various other facets of my life. As she watched me dance in the back of the church, it was as if God had placed her at the gates of my destiny. She has impacted my journey greatly through her consistent prayer, encouragement, correction, guidance, love, hearing from the Lord concerning my life, covering my ministry, building me in character and honor and this list could go on for quite a while. Very early on in my destiny journey, God released her to my life to help steer me on the path and protect me. We are doing life together with destinies that are connected by God's design. Not only was she released to me, I was released to her as well. Just as Mordecai was a blessing to Esther's life, Esther was also a blessing to his and it is an honor to have this type of rare relationship in my life. It is one to be treasured and is essential to each person seeing the will of God unfold in their life.

Not everybody can be an apostolic governor of your life and that is okay because not everyone is equipped and designed to handle that calling. We must discern who those people are so that we can acquire all that God has designed for us to receive from them. This is also key so that we do not have people in positions within our lives that they are not called to which can be harmful to both them and you.

They may not be called to:
- ✓ The unique vision, destiny, and calling that is on your life
- ✓ The sleepless nights and time that it takes to guard and cover you
- ✓ The warfare and the demonic assignments set against you
- ✓ The attentiveness, care, and observance that is necessary
- ✓ The ability to counsel, guide, and charge (command) you
- ✓ The time and work it takes to cultivate a relationship with you that embodies the attributes of love, respect, submission, value, obedience, and honor
- ✓ The level of engagement and interaction that is needed
- ✓ Marrying the vision of another and what it takes to walk in true covenant relationship in destiny and calling

There have been times people drew to me, but were not God appointed as governors of my life. As I took the time to pray about them, God would give me visions and dreams, clearly tell me no or yes, show me they were not headed in the direction of his vision for me, and more. They were good, nice, and anointed people, but God had not set them in my life as a mentor or governor. When this happens, it is perfectly okay because even though we may have desires and great love for a person, we can only be who God has called and ordained us to be in a person's life. I learned how to engage people from a place that is healthy, balanced, and does not make them or myself more than what God said. I do not begin new relationships without the leading of the Lord and taking the time pray about its purpose and position in my life. God has given me peace about interacting with those who are drawn to me from a place of truth to not cause any harm to myself and them.

The apostolic governors that God has ordained for your life will not have to be told what to do and where they need to be to adequately cover you. They will already be abiding with you, and will have already prepared the way for you. THEY LIVE THE JOURNEY WITH YOU AND ESTABLISH THEMSELVES AT THE GATES OF YOUR DESTINY!

> ***Esther 2:21-23*** *In those days, as Mordecai was sitting at the king's gate, Bigthan and Teresh, two of the king's eunuchs, who guarded the threshold, became angry and sought to lay hands on King Ahasuerus. And this came to the knowledge of Mordecai, and he told it to Queen Esther, and Esther told the king in the name of Mordecai. When the affair was investigated and found to be so, the men were both hanged on the gallows. And it was recorded in the book of the chronicles in the presence of the king.*

While positioned at the king's gate, Mordecai and discovered Bigthan and Teresh's (the king's chamberlains and doorkeepers) plot to kill the king. This is very interesting because Bigthan and Teresh were the doorkeepers and they were the breach in their own security. Had the king been killed it would have interfered with Esther's position as queen and subsequently altered Mordecai's position as well. Bigthan and Teresh thought that they would be able to infiltrate the gate because they were the guards; but when Esther was announced as queen and Mordecai took his seat at the gate, the guards had been changed. Mordecai was at the gate in secret ambush so as the attacks began to arise, he was there to immediately thwart them. This is what the apostolic governors of our lives do, they are like the stealth bombers over our destiny. They sit in silent ambush at our gates, discover the enemy's plans before they hit, exercise influence over what occurs concerning us, and then frustrate the plans of the enemy.

> ***Esther 3:1-2 English Standard Version*** *After these things King Ahasuerus promoted Haman the Agagite, the son of Hammedatha, and advanced him and set his throne above all the officials who were with him. And all the king's servants who were at the king's gate bowed down and paid homage to Haman, for the king had so commanded concerning him. But Mordecai did not bow down or pay homage.*

Haman was promoted above the other officials and because of his position, all the servants at the king's gate bowed. Bowing to Haman would have been sin and idolatry, therefore, Mordecai kept his post and did not bow. Bowing to an authority other than God would have changed his posture at the gate since your head is down and your vision is obstructed when you bow. As a result, he would have submitted his vision to Haman. It is important that those who govern the gates of our lives do not bow to the enemy and fall into sin. If they do, they shift their alignment and come under the submission of another vision. Since they are governing us, they shift our alignment as well. This is reason we cannot serve two masters, because whatever you bow to requires your loyalty (Matthew 6:24).

Had Mordecai bowed to Haman:

- ✓ He would have been saying that he respected his laws, and was in agreement with them, thus relinquishing his governing power at the gates to Haman
- ✓ His entire vision would have changed
- ✓ Haman would have become Mordecai's god
- ✓ The laws and vision of Haman would have exalted above the law and vision of God
- ✓ He would have come into agreement with the death decree against him and his people, giving it free entrance to come right in and take over
- ✓ He would have been serving Haman rather than serving God
- ✓ He would have been operating outside of true purpose at the gate. This is important because many times we are positioned where we are supposed to be in destiny, but due to bowing and succumbing to ungodliness we operate outside of our true purpose for being there

The scripture said that "all the **king's servants** that

were at the king's gates, bowed." It was normal custom to bow to high officials and royalty at the king's gate, but Mordecai was not a king's servant; he was **God's**. He was stationed at the gate to govern and keep watch over Esther. Apostolic governors commit to remain free of conformity and stay focused on the true purpose of our positions.

> **Romans 12:2** *And be not conformed to this world: but be ye transformed by the renewing of your mind, that ye may prove what is that good, and acceptable, and perfect, will of God.*
>
> **Esther 3:3-6** *Then the king's servants who were at the king's gate said to Mordecai, "Why do you transgress the king's command?" And when they spoke to him day after day and he would not listen to them, they told Haman, in order to see whether Mordecai's words would stand, for he had told them that he was a Jew. And when Haman saw that Mordecai did not bow down or pay homage to him, Haman was filled with fury. But he disdained to lay hands on Mordecai alone. So, as they had made known to him the people of Mordecai, Haman sought to destroy all the Jews, the people of Mordecai, throughout the whole kingdom of Ahasuerus.*

The king's servants recognized that Mordecai was not bowing and informed Haman. They wanted to see if Mordecai would continue to stand so they could question his actions. It was as if the enemy was now stalking Mordecai to find an opening to entrap him. When we stand as firm governors, the enemy will sometimes send stalking spirits to watch us. Apostolic governors need to be aware of seasons where the enemy is watching and trying to gain information about them. Even as the enemy is watching, do not lose focus or move out of your position. My spiritual mother consistently stands firm in who she is in God, to me, and the standards of God for my life. One time I did business with a company that did not provide me with the best quality of work and was not willing to work with me on producing the vision I wanted the product to display. Very politely, I expressed this and did not receive a response that was of this same manner and character. The interactions became very hostile and resistant although it was my heart to reach the end goal of a good quality product and not offend anyone in the process. I continually expressed this and started to settle for something that was not the original product. As I shared this with my spiritual mother, she immediately told me that I was not to settle and God was using this to teach me how to be confrontational (of course with integrity and honor) such that the fullness of his standard of excellence upon me would manifest all the more. I applied her advice and ended up not being able to work with the company on the product. What came of this decision was alignment with another group who was willing and had the heart to embody the vision God gave me. My spiritual mother stood firmly with me in the standard of excellence God was holding me too. This was a character shaping experience as confidence, boldness, and intentionality in not settling for anything less than God's will was built in me.

Haman was so enraged by Mordecai that he released a death sentence for the Jews within all the provinces. He sought to kill and destroy an entire generation and remnant of people who were set apart servants of God not subject to his demonic rule. They deflated his false reality of ruler-ship, and he was infuriated by what he could not control. Therefore, he formed a mission to kill them all. The enemy will seek to kill those who are like us, connected to us, a part of our remnant and generational lineage because of what we represent. He wants to stop our ability to multiply and increase in the earth because he sees our greater power and authority.

> ***Esther 4:1-4*** *When Mordecai perceived all that was done, Mordecai rent his clothes, and put on sackcloth with ashes, and went out into the midst of the city, and cried with a loud and a bitter cry; And came even before the king's gate: for none might enter into the king's gate clothed with sackcloth. And in every province, whithersoever the king's commandment and his decree came, there was great mourning among the Jews, and fasting, and weeping, and wailing; and many lay in sackcloth and ashes.*
>
> *So Esther's maids and her chamberlains came and told it her. Then was the queen exceedingly grieved; and she sent raiment to clothe Mordecai, and to take away his sackcloth from him: but he received it not.*

After Mordecai found out about the decree of death

against him and his people, he was immediately grieved. In the chapter on Nehemiah, his first response was also to grieve, and this provoked change. Mordecai rent his clothes and put on sackcloth with ashes which was customary of those who were mourning. He went out about the city crying and sat before the gate mourning. These were not normal cries; they were cries of intercession. He went all around the city with intercessory cries, and then went out before the gate wearing sackcloth. Because Jewish law prohibited him from entering the gate while mourning, he stood at the threshold and made intercession for his people.

Cried in the Strong's of this scripture means:

1. To announce or convene publicly
2. Assemble, call together
3. Come with such a company, gather together
4. Cause to be proclaimed
5. To cry, cry out, call, call for help
6. To be called together, be joined together
7. To make a crying proclaim
8. To have a proclamation made
9. To call out to, to call out at

As Mordecai was crying, he was calling out to the Lord for his divine intervention. He was summoning God and the host of heaven to be assembled together to deliver them.

As we apostolically govern, we must make sure that we do not fall into depression, defeat, and despair. We should use that grief as a strategy and release cries of intercession. If our cries are filled with purpose and action for change, they are profoundly powerful. Our grieving cries should **INVOKE** and **INCITE** God to move.

Sidebar Revelation: King David would often cry out to the Lord in intercession during his challenging destiny journey because he knew that God would hear him, answer, and deliver.

> *Psalms 18:6-19 In my distress I called upon the Lord, and cried unto my God: he heard my voice out of his temple, and my cry came before him, even into his ears. Then the earth shook and trembled; the foundations also of the hills moved and were shaken, because he was wroth. There went up a smoke out of his nostrils, and fire out of his mouth devoured: coals were kindled by it. He bowed the heavens also, and came down: and darkness was under his feet. And he rode upon a cherub, and did fly: yea, he did fly upon the wings of the wind. He made darkness his secret place; his pavilion round about him were dark waters and thick clouds of the skies. At the brightness that was before him his thick clouds passed, hail stones and coals of fire. The Lord also thundered in the heavens, and the Highest gave his voice; hail stones and coals of fire. Yea, he sent out his arrows, and scattered them; and he shot out lightnings, and discomfited them. Then the channels of waters were seen, and the foundations of the world were discovered at thy rebuke, O Lord, at the blast of the breath of thy nostrils. He sent from above, he took me, he drew me out of many waters. He delivered me from my strong enemy, and from*

them which hated me: for they were too strong for me. They prevented me in the day of my calamity: but the Lord was my stay. He brought me forth also into a large place; he delivered me, because he delighted in me.

From this scriptural passage we learn that as we intercede through crying:

- ✓ Our cries reach the temple of the Lord
- ✓ Our cries go before the Lord and enter into his ears
- ✓ Our cries kindle the anger of the Lord and cause the earth to shake, tremble, and the foundations of the hills to be moved
- ✓ Our cries cause the judgment of the Lord to be released on our behalf - fiery judgment smoke is released from his nostrils, devouring fire is released from his mouth, hail stones and coals of fire are released from his clouds
- ✓ Our cries cause heaven to descend and invite God to come in - he bowed the heavens and came down, and he thunders from heaven
- ✓ Our cries cause the arsenal of the Lord to be opened - he sent out his arrows, and scattered them, he shot out lightning's, released the blast of his nostrils
- ✓ Our cries bring deliverance - he delivered me from my strong enemy and for those who hated me and were too strong for me
- ✓ Our cries invite God's limitless almighty strength and support
- ✓ Our cries bring forth his delight in us

Mordecai's cries to the Lord reached heaven and pulled down strategy to annihilate the wicked decree against the Jews.

> **Esther 4:4** *So Esther's maids and her chamberlains came and told it her. Then was the queen exceedingly grieved; and she sent raiment to clothe Mordecai, and to take away his sackcloth from him: but he received it not.*

Esther learned about Mordecai grieving, and sent raiment (clothing) to him, but he did not receive it. Although her intentions were to care for him, she was essentially covering up the problem rather than delivering a solution for it. She was the sent one for this time, but instead of presenting herself, she sent clothes in her place. Mordecai's cries at the gate had a purpose, so he could not accept the garments because it would have moved him from his position of intercession. He would have been clothing himself with the problem and enmeshing with it, rather than standing in opposition against it to be destroyed. At this time, Esther did not know of the death decree that had been released against the Jewish people, so she was operating from a place of her heart with good intentions rather than the truth of what was going on, and what was truly necessary at the time. She was right in the midst of the attack, and did not even know it. This is reason we need those who can help us to govern our destiny because there will be times where attacks are set against us that we are unaware of. When we see those who are covering us in intense states of warfare and intercession, it will be our heart and intention to make them feel better, but it is key to the fulfillment of our destiny that they remain in that place of intercession. We must quickly shift and grasp the true revelation so that we too can get in our position. Being the main armor-bearer to my spiritual mother, I walk through seasons of warfare with her firsthand. Out of my love for her I would want to kill every devil and cause these seasons to end. This would always bring me into a place of engaging the warfare through my emotions and heart. God had to teach me how to quickly shift from my heart to my spirit, where the supernatural strength of the Lord resides, and where I would be able to empower and cover her most effectively. This helped me focus on the assignment rather than creating another one. Once I got this revelation, my armor-bearing abilities shifted to a whole new dimension of depth and power.

> ***Esther 4:5-9 English Standard Version*** *Then Esther called for Hathach, one of the king's eunuchs, who had been appointed to attend her, and ordered him to go to Mordecai to learn what this was and why it was. Hathach went out to Mordecai in the open square of the city in front of the king's gate, and Mordecai told him all that had happened to him, and the exact sum of money that Haman had promised to pay into the king's treasuries for the destruction of the Jews. Mordecai also gave him a copy of the written decree issued in Susa for their destruction, that he might show it to Esther and explain it to her and command her to go to the king to beg his favor and plead with him on behalf of her people. And Hathach went and told Esther what*

Mordecai had said.

Esther learned the truth about the plans of Haman to destroy all the Jews and Mordecai once again charges her to go to the next level of her destiny shift. He knew the power of her position and could see the influence that she had. The apostolic governors of our lives will continuously encourage us to go higher because they see the need for who we are. They know the influence, favor, authority, and power that we will have as we launch forward.

Mordecai gave Esther a copy of the decree Haman created and told her how should help her people. He did not just say "come on Esther, do something!" He gave her the demonic decree so she would be knowledgeable of the enemy's plan and he encouraged her to ask the king for his favor. The apostolic governors helping us through destiny will know what our shift looks like and will give clear instructions and strategic plans on how to execute it. They will not expose us and push us forward to fend for ourselves with no direction. They counsel and guide us in alignment with God.

> **Esther 4:10-14** *Then Esther spoke to Hathach and commanded him to go to Mordecai and say, "All the king's servants and the people of the king's provinces know that if any man or woman goes to the king inside the inner court without being called, there is but one law – to be put to death, except the one to whom the king holds out the golden scepter so that he may live. But as for me, I*

have not been called to come in to the king these thirty days."

And they told Mordecai what Esther had said. Then Mordecai told them to reply to Esther, "Do not think to yourself that in the king's palace you will escape any more than all the other Jews. For if you keep silent at this time, relief and deliverance will rise for the Jews from another place, but you and your father's house will perish. And who knows whether you have not come to the kingdom for such a time as this?"

After hearing the direction of Mordecai, Esther responded through her fear and tells him of the custom that is followed when approaching the king. She is not aware that because she is God's chosen queen she would have limitless favor to fulfill her destiny assignment. Although she grew up being obedient to the instructions of Mordecai, this instruction was different than the others because of the dangers it presented. Despite Esther's reserves, Mordecai speaks truth to her. If she did not arise she would not escape the attack against the Jews, deliverance would come in another form, but she and her family would be destroyed. He told her to not think that just because she was in the palace she would be able to escape. Many times we are right where we need to be in destiny but out of fear we hold back.

We think the position of destiny itself will save us, and that merely being a part of a ministry, a good church, or having delegated duties will save us, but it will not. Only genuine engagement with destiny and fulfilling purpose will save us and bring us under its covering and protection. It is the fulfillment of our very purpose that will destroy our enemies. Within our destiny we are specifically assigned to certain enemies that only we can take out. Only David could take out Goliath, only Moses could take out Pharaoh, only Jesus could crush the power of sin and utterly destroy the works of the devil, and only Esther could do this work.

As we govern we are not to be merely present in ministries or churches that give us opportunity. We are to be active in functioning in our God-ordained destiny and purpose for being there. Regions, territories, generations, and lives are contingent upon our destiny, and whether or not we shift out of being a part of it to indeed walking and fulfilling our purpose within it. The apostolic governors of our lives are those who will speak truth to us and will not sugar coat or hold their tongue about the urgency and desperate need for us to launch forward.

We need them so that:

- ✓ We do not sit on destiny and stand right in the midst of it yet produce no fruit
- ✓ We do not live in opportunity and what could potentially be
- ✓ We are not just merely a part of ministries and churches, but we are functioning in our God-ordained purpose for the advancement of the Kingdom of God

- ✓ We do not become stagnate in our walk, becoming familiar with position but void of purpose
- ✓ We do not waste the favor and the open doors that are upon our lives
- ✓ We do not succumb to fear of what will happen if we step out against the norms
- ✓ God does not have to send someone else to do what he has originally pre-appointed us to do
- ✓ They can continually push us forward in destiny, and speak truth to us- even the hard things, and empower us
- ✓ They can open our eyes and expand our vision to see the fullness of who we are and who God has called us to be

> ***Esther 4:15-17 English Standard Version*** *Then Esther told them to reply to Mordecai, "Go, gather all the Jews to be found in Susa, and hold a fast on my behalf, and do not eat or drink for three days, night or day. I and my young women will also fast as you do. Then I will go to the king, though it is against the law, and if I perish, I perish." Mordecai then went away and did everything as Esther had ordered him.*

Esther embraced the shift and asked for the other Jews and her maidens too fast to cover her assignment. She acknowledged she could potentially face the penalty of death, but completing her assignment to save her people was more prominent to her than her own life. Apostolic governors are not afraid of the penalties that may come against them, even if the penalty is death. Fulfilling their purpose is

priority.

Our calling and assignment may cause us to oppose traditional systems and defy religious practices. When this is no longer a source of fear that causes us to waver against God's instructions, this is proof that we are ready to break through the barrier of those customs to complete our assignment.

> ***Esther 5:1-3*** *Now it came to pass on the third day, that Esther put on her royal apparel, and stood in the inner court of the king's house, over against the king's house:and the king sat upon his royal throne in the royal house, over against the gate of the house. And it was so, when the king saw Esther the queen standing in the court, that she obtained favour in his sight:and the king held out to Esther the golden sceptre that was in his hand. So Esther drew near, and touched the top of the sceptre. Then said the king unto her, What wilt thou, queen Esther? and what is thy request? it shall be even given thee to the half of the kingdom.*

Esther put on the garments of her royal apparel and stood in the inner court of the king's house like she had become clothed for the assignment. The king welcomed her to come to him which is symbolic of how God favors and treats us as we align and walk in destiny and purpose, and as we boldly approach him knowing who we are. When we come before God and express what we are needing, he immediately gives us favor and provides us with even more than what we have asked for. The king told Esther that she could have half of his kingdom if that is what she wanted. This type of favor was only presented to her as she began genuinely walking in fulfilling her purpose. Being aligned in destiny and purpose will activate the favor that we need to advance.

> ***Esther 5:4-14 English Standard Version*** *And Esther said, "If it please the king, let the king and Haman come today to a feast that I have prepared for the king." Then the king said, "Bring Haman quickly, so that we may do as Esther has asked." So the king and Haman came to the feast that Esther had prepared. And as they were drinking wine after the feast, the king said to Esther, "What is your wish? It shall be granted you. And what is your request? Even to the half of my kingdom, it shall be fulfilled." Then Esther answered, "My wish and my request is: If I have found favor in the sight of the king, and if it please the king to grant my wish and fulfill my request, let the king and Haman come to the feast that I will prepare for them, and tomorrow I will do as the king has said."*
>
> *And Haman went out that day joyful and glad of heart. But when Haman saw Mordecai in the king's gate, that he neither rose nor trembled before him, he was filled with wrath against Mordecai. Nevertheless, Haman restrained himself and went home, and he sent and brought his friends and his wife Zeresh. And Haman recounted to them the splendor of his riches, the number of his sons, all the promotions with which the king had honored him, and how he had advanced him above the officials and the servants of the king. Then Haman said, "Even Queen Esther let no one but me come with*

> *the king to the feast she prepared. And tomorrow also I am invited by her together with the king. Yet all this is worth nothing to me, so long as I see Mordecai the Jew sitting at the king's gate." Then his wife Zeresh and all his friends said to him, "Let a gallows fifty cubits high be made, and in the morning tell the king to have Mordecai hanged upon it. Then go joyfully with the king to the feast." This idea pleased Haman, and he had the gallows made.*

Esther asked for the king and Haman to come to a banquet that she would prepare for them and then the next day she would tell them her request. She was patient, discerning, and slow to use wisdom for the right timing to release her request when it would be most effective. After the banquet, Haman was joyful and glad because he had met with the king and queen and he was feeling good about himself. On his way home as he passed by the king's gate, he saw Mordecai and once again Mordecai did not bow. The scripture says that "he was full of indignation against Mordecai."

<u>*Indignation*</u> in the Strong's in this scripture means:

1. Heat
2. Anger, poison
3. Anger, bottles, hot displeasure
4. Furious, rage, wrath
5. Fever
6. Venom, poison
7. Burning anger, rage

When Haman saw Mordecai standing in his

unrelenting position at the gates, he was HOT! Mordecai's stance literally made him sick and feverish. Wow! It is powerful to know that our stance in destiny makes the devil sick and is like poisonous venom to him. As we keep standing unwaveringly, he is filled with hot displeasure, fury, burning anger, and rage, and cannot do anything about it.

After seeing Mordecai, Haman went home and called for his friends so that he could brag about his riches and fortunes. He was knocked off of his arrogant high horse, so he tried to soothe his ego through the flattery of his friends. Our destiny stance makes the devil feel inferior, insecure, and intimidated so much that he has to find ways to inflate himself. As Haman was bragging about all of his possessions he says, "Yet all this availeth me nothing, so long as I see Mordecai the Jew sitting at the king's gate."

Availeth in the Strong's in this scripture means:

1. To level, equalize
2. To resemble, to adjust
3. Bring forth, compare, counteravail
4. Equal, profit
5. To agree with, be or become like, level, resemble
6. To be like, equivalent
7. To level, smooth
8. To make like, to be alike

As long as Mordecai was sitting at the king's gate none of Haman's riches meant anything. Mordecai was above any comparison to Haman's possessions because his destiny superseded all that Haman had. He knew that Mordecai was beyond him, and the devil also knows that we are beyond him. Consequently, he aims to kill us in an attempt to level the ground, smooth it out, adjust, and equalize things, because as long as we exist there is no comparison. There is no equality between us and the devil.

Haman's friends tell him to have gallows created which is a post used for hanging. They created a weapon specifically for killing Mordecai. The enemy will form weapons specifically for killing us, but Isaiah 54:17 says, "No weapon that is formed against thee shall prosper; and every tongue that shall rise against thee in judgement thou shalt condemn. This is the heritage of the servants of the Lord, and their righteousness is of me, saith the Lord."

No weapon formed will be successful or profitable against us!

Condemn in the Strong's in this scripture means:

1. To disturb, violate
2. Make trouble, vex
3. To be guilty, be condemned
4. To condemn as guilty (in civil relations)
5. To act wickedly (in ethics and religion)

Every demonic tongue and weapon that rises against us we disturb, vex, violate, and judge as wicked and guilty!

Heritage in the Strong's in this scripture means:

1. Something inherited, occupancy, an heirloom
2. Generally an estate, patrimony or portion
3. Possession, property, inheritance, heritage
4. Portion, share

Condemning, judging, and overpowering the weapons of the enemy is our inheritance, portion, and estate. We are heirs to the throne of judgment!

As weapons are specifically made for us, they become impotent and of no effect against us!

Haman's friends told him to let the gallows be made 50 cubits high which is equivalent to 73 feet high. That level of height is symbolic of how arrogant and puffed up Haman was.

> **Esther 6:1-12 English Standard Version** *On that night the king could not sleep. And he gave orders to bring the book of memorable deeds, the chronicles, and they were read before the king. And it was found written how Mordecai had told about Bigthana and Teresh, two of the king's eunuchs, who guarded the threshold, and who had sought to lay hands on King Ahasuerus. And the king said, "What honor or distinction has been bestowed on Mordecai for this?" The king's young men who attended him said, "Nothing has been done for him." And the king said, "Who is in the court?" Now Haman had just entered the outer court of the king's palace to speak to the king about having Mordecai hanged on the gallows that he had prepared for him. And the king's young men told him, "Haman is there, standing in the court." And the king said, "Let him come in."*

So Haman came in, and the king said to him, "What should be done to the man whom the king delights to honor?" And Haman said to himself, "Whom would the king delight to honor more than me?" And Haman said to the king, "For the man whom the king delights to honor, let royal robes be brought, which the king has worn, and the horse that the king has ridden, and on whose head a royal crown is set. And let the robes and the horse be handed over to one of the king's most noble officials. Let them dress the man whom the king delights to honor, and let them lead him on the horse through the square of the city, proclaiming before him: 'Thus shall it be done to the man whom the king delights to honor.'" Then the king said to Haman, "Hurry; take the robes and the horse, as you have said, and do so to Mordecai the Jew, who sits at the king's gate. Leave out nothing that you have mentioned." So Haman took the robes and the horse, and he dressed Mordecai and led him through the square of the city, proclaiming before him, "Thus shall it be done to the man whom the king delights to honor." Then Mordecai returned to the king's gate. But Haman hurried to his house, mourning and with his head covered.

The king could not sleep that night so he had the book of records read to him. He heard in the records that Mordecai had saved his life and is informed that nothing had been done to compensate Mordecai, so he planned to honor him. It is God's divine timing that the king was unable to sleep, and that he would come across the records of the good acts of Mordecai at that exact time. Haman was waiting in the outer court to talk to the king about hanging Mordecai, but the king already had it in his heart to bless and honor Mordecai. While our enemies plan to kill us, God will plan to bless and honor us. As we apostolically govern destiny we must know that no matter how many times the enemy plans against us, God's plans for us will always prevail over the enemies and triumph on our behalf.

Haman came into the inner court with the king and was asked "what should be done to the man who he delighted to honor?" Because Haman was filled with so much pride, it had become self-idolatry. His level of self-absorption caused him to assume the king meant to honor him. The king announced that he delighted to honor Mordecai the Jew and Haman is utterly humiliated. After Haman paraded Mordecai through the city, he ran home covering himself to hide the embarrassment. God will shame our enemies and make them honor and bless us. If we do not bow to the enemy and we stand strong, eventually he will be subject to us.

> ***Esther 7:1-10 English Standard Version*** *So the king and Haman went in to feast with Queen Esther. And on the second day, as they were drinking wine after the feast, the king again said to Esther, "What is your wish, Queen Esther? It shall be granted you. And what is your request? Even to the half of my kingdom, it shall be fulfilled." Then Queen Esther answered, "If I have found favor in your sight, O king, and if it please the king, let my life be granted me for my wish, and my people for my request. For we have been sold, I and my people,*

to be destroyed, to be killed, and to be annihilated. If we had been sold merely as slaves, men and women, I would have been silent, for our affliction is not to be compared with the loss to the king." Then King Ahasuerus said to Queen Esther, "Who is he, and where is he, who has dared to do this?" And Esther said, "A foe and enemy! This wicked Haman!" Then Haman was terrified before the king and the queen.

And the king arose in his wrath from the wine-drinking and went into the palace garden, but Haman stayed to beg for his life from Queen Esther, for he saw that harm was determined against him by the king. And the king returned from the palace garden to the place where they were drinking wine, as Haman was falling on the couch where Esther was. And the king said, "Will he even assault the queen in my presence, in my own house?" As the word left the mouth of the king, they covered Haman's face. Then Harbona, one of the eunuchs in attendance on the king, said, "Moreover, the gallows that Haman has prepared for Mordecai, whose word saved the king, is standing at Haman's house, fifty cubits high." And the king said, "Hang him on that." So they hanged Haman on the gallows that he had prepared for Mordecai. Then the wrath of the king abated.

Esther asked the king that her life and the lives of her people be spared from destruction, and he is angry as he hears about the decree against her and her people. He is even more infuriated when he learns that Haman was the planner of the attack. Haman was terrified and begged for his life from Esther, but the death that he planned for Mordecai became his own death. The judgements that the enemy releases against us are his own fate. Whatever weapons he forms against us, are the very weapons that we can strategically use against him. This is the heritage of apostolic governors.

> ***Esther 8:3-6 English Standard Version*** *Then Esther spoke again to the king. She fell at his feet and wept and pleaded with him to avert the evil plan of Haman the Agagite and the plot that he had devised against the Jews. When the king held out the golden scepter to Esther, Esther rose and stood before the king. And she said, "If it please the king, and if I have found favor in his sight, and if the thing seems right before the king, and I am pleasing in his eyes, let an order be written to revoke the letters devised by Haman the Agagite, the son of Hammedatha, which he wrote to destroy the Jews who are in all the provinces of the king. For how can I bear to see the calamity that is coming to my people? Or how can I bear to see the destruction of my kindred?"*

Although Haman was dead, the death decree was still in effect so Esther's work was not yet complete. She approached the king again with another request to reverse the letters devised by Haman. As we govern effectively, when we reach one place of victory we have to continue going forward to obtain full victory. We must do a complete reversal and cover all bases to make sure nothing is lingering and the assignment is completely finished.

> *Esther 8:10-14 English Standard Version And he wrote in the name of King Ahasuerus and sealed it with the king's signet ring. Then he sent the letters by mounted couriers riding on swift horses that were used in the king's service, bred from the royal stud, saying that the king allowed the Jews who were in every city to gather and defend their lives, to destroy, to kill, and to annihilate any armed force of any people or province that might attack them, children and women included, and to plunder their goods, on one day throughout all the provinces of King Ahasuerus, on the thirteenth day of the twelfth month, which is the month of Adar. A copy of what was written was to be issued as a decree in every province, being publicly displayed to all peoples, and the Jews were to be ready on that day to take vengeance on their enemies. So the couriers, mounted on their swift horses that were used in the king's service, rode out hurriedly, urged by the king's command. And the decree was issued in Susa the citadel.*

The Jewish people were granted the ability to stand against the armed forces that would attack them on the designated date of the decree. There could have been a reversal written to cancel the attack, but this reversal decree gave the Jews legal authority to kill and destroy their enemies. The decree against the Jews worked in their favor to expose their enemies because the armed forces were not expecting the Jews to be ready to fight and defend themselves.

> *Esther 9:3-5 All the officials of the provinces and the satraps and the governors and the royal agents*

> *also helped the Jews, for the fear of Mordecai had fallen on them. For Mordecai was great in the king's house, and his fame spread throughout all the provinces, for the man Mordecai grew more and more powerful. The Jews struck all their enemies with the sword, killing and destroying them, and did as they pleased to those who hated them.*

Mordecai became great in the king's house and all of the provinces. He is an example of an apostolic governor who walks as a spiritual parent, leader, and gatekeeper of destiny in strong godly covenant, honor, and never-ending devotion to the stance of God for his life. Who he was, was divinely connected to empowering Esther. He is a true depiction of humility, as he was meek to the will and vision of the Lord for Esther's life. Through his relentless covering and guidance, an entire people group and multiple generations were saved. Mordecai's name means "little man", but the little man humble and solely submitted to God was a powerful apostolic governing force.

Prayer:

In this season of your life let divine connections with those who God has ordained to be a part of your destiny and calling journey come forth. Those who have a specific appointing and anointing to be able to help you govern over who you are in the Lord, give you guidance, speak truth to you, and push you in going forward in what God is requiring of you and calling you to do. Those who are sold out to serving the Lord in their destiny and calling and are bowed to only Jesus. Let these connections be your portion in this season to help you, to stand at the gates of your destiny, and do life with you. Shift even now to becoming actively engaged in walking in your destiny and overthrowing the demonic plans and assignments of the enemy that are sent against you and those around you. You are no longer merely in position in the correct place for destiny, in a good ministry, and a part of a good church. You are shifting to walking in purpose. Decreeing that Mordecai's are arising in this season and are being led to those whom God has set to be under your watch and care. Through these covenant relationships destinies are coming forth, and the kingdom of God is being advanced. In Jesus name, Amen!

Chapter 3

Reflection Questions

1. *Do you have a spiritual mother, father, leader, who is an apostolic governor in your life? Write about them as it relates to what you have learned from this chapter?*

2. *Do you walk in an "every day" established covenant relationship with your spiritual parent or leader? Are there areas where you know you need to be more devoted to the relationship?*

3. *Rate yourself from 1-10, 10 being the best on the 5 attributes of relationship listed in this chapter. (Respect, honor, value, submission, obedience.)*

4. *Are you holding back in any ways and not going forward in your purpose? What are the fears that hold you back? Journal these and place them before God. Ask him to fill you with his truth about who he has purposed you to be.*

5. *"It is the fulfillment of our very purpose that will destroy our enemies." This is a quote from this chapter. What enemies are you specifically assigned to take out? It is okay if you do not know this now. You can journal your thoughts on this question and ask God to reveal this to you.*

6. *Are there areas of your destiny you know you need to launch forth in at this time?*

7. *Have fulfilling God's purpose for your life become what is most prominent to you? How can you relinquish your will more so that you can receive God's will for you?*

Chapter 4
Samson: Opportunity Based Destiny vs. Lifestyle Based Destiny

When exploring the life of Samson will teach us about the importance of having clear vision of who we are and being intentional in carrying out our divine purpose. Samson is a prime example of someone who had great destiny **moments** by the Spirit of the Lord filling him on occasion, but not one who habitually communed with the Holy Spirit to be directed through his journey. He endured multiple downfalls that ultimately cost him his life because he was not a responsible governor of God's vision for him. We need clear vision of who we are as apostolic governors, and be devoted to the standards God has given us that protect and help bring to pass the fullness of his vision for our lives.

> *Judges 13:2-7 English Standard Version There was a certain man of Zorah, of the tribe of the Danites, whose name was Manoah. And his wife was barren and had no children. And the angel of the Lord appeared to the woman and said to her, "Behold, you are barren and have not borne children, but you shall conceive and bear a son. Therefore be careful and drink no wine or strong drink, and eat nothing unclean, for behold, you shall conceive and bear a son. No razor shall come upon his head, for the child shall be a Nazirite to God from the womb, and he shall begin to save Israel from the hand of the Philistines." Then the woman came and told her husband, "A man of God came to*

> *me, and his appearance was like the appearance of the angel of God, very awesome. I did not ask him where he was from, and he did not tell me his name, but he said to me, Behold, you shall conceive and bear a son. So then drink no wine or strong drink, and eat nothing unclean, for the child shall be a Nazirite to God from the womb to the day of his death.'"*

God gave clear specific instructions for how Samson was to be nurtured in the womb, how he was to be raised, and how he was to continue to live until his death. As Samson became an adult, he needed to be personally accountable to following these instructions as they were not just for his mother and father. In this angelic visitation, God gave Samson's mother vision of his purpose to save Israel from the Philistines. He is called a Nazarite- one consecrated, set apart, and devoted to the purposes and services of the Lord. She had to be cautious of what she consumed, so she could not drink any wine or eat anything unclean. His hair also could never be cut. These instructions were an important part of his Nazarite nature, and empowered him in the purpose of God for his life. He was to belong to the Lord, and be devoted to the saving of his people. However, as we continue to read the story of his life, it is surprising how so little of his life was set apart to fulfilling the Lord's vision.

From our birth, we were given a divine purpose and vision from the Lord for our lives. These are standards that we need to be responsible for that protect and endow us with the supernatural power and abilities we need to fulfill our assignments. These standards will sometimes increase as we mature and go deeper in our calling. Even though we may not be a Nazarite in the traditional sense like Samson, we need to be Nazarites in respect to the specific vision, standards, and purposes of the Lord for our lives. Parents should develop this mindset and seek God for revelation in this area to help govern and teach their children how to walk in destiny. Parents are the first governors of our lives. They set our foundations and create the basis for our journey. From our birth, they should pray and seek God for who we are, what we are called to do, and what his destiny plan is for us, so they can steer and guide us in alignment with our design. Their paramount influence in our lives is a strong shaping force.

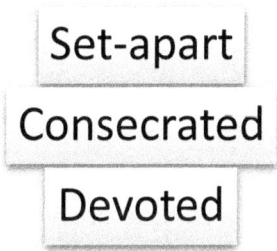

Judges 14:1-4 English Standard Version Samson went down to Timnah, and at Timnah he saw one of the daughters of the Philistines. Then he came up and told his father and mother, "I saw one of the daughters of the Philistines at Timnah. Now get her for me as my wife." But his father and mother said to him, "Is there not a woman among the daughters of your relatives, or among all our people, that you must go to take a wife from

> the uncircumcised Philistines?" But Samson said to his father, "Get her for me, for she is right in my eyes." His father and mother did not know that it was from the LORD, for he was seeking an opportunity against the Philistines. At that time the Philistines ruled over Israel.

Samson expressed his desire to marry a Philistine woman and his parents immediately opposed the idea. It almost seemed as if they were more careful with the instructions of the Lord for his life than he was. Perhaps they had not been tested in passing the baton from their accountability to allowing their son to be responsible for his destiny. This can be a challenge of finding the balance of sometimes watching children make mistakes without interfering. Otherwise, they are obedient but their heart is not in agreement. Samson's parents knew that it was his purpose to kill the Philistines, and it was not customary for an Israelite to marry a Philistine since they were at war with one another. Although the scripture does say that "it was of the Lord, that he sought an occasion against the Philistines," we do not know if Samson was aware that God was using this as a chance to attack against the Philistines, or if his focus alone was solely in marrying the Philistine woman. This is a key point! If we are completely devoted to walking in our destiny and calling, the work of our assignments should not be done through opportunity and random occurrences in our lives. It should be a part of us. God should be able to guide us where we are purposely involved in our destiny.

We should be partnering with God and the Holy Spirit to fulfill the call on our lives, and not be opportunity based, but lifestyle-based.

> ***Judges 14:5-14 English Standard Version*** *Then Samson went down with his father and mother to Timnah, and they came to the vineyards of Timnah. And behold, a young lion came toward him roaring. Then the Spirit of the LORD rushed upon him, and although he had nothing in his hand, he tore the lion in pieces as one tears a young goat. But he did not tell his father or his mother what he had done. Then he went down and talked with the woman, and she was right in Samson's eyes.*
>
> *After some days he returned to take her. And he turned aside to see the carcass of the lion, and behold, there was a swarm of bees in the body of the lion, and honey. He scraped it out into his hands and went on, eating as he went. And he came to his father and mother and gave some to them, and they ate. But he did not tell them that he had scraped the honey from the carcass of the lion.*
>
> *His father went down to the woman, and Samson prepared a feast there, for so the young men used to do. As soon as the people saw him, they brought thirty companions to be with him. And Samson said to them, "Let me now put a riddle to you. If you can tell me what it is, within the seven days of the feast, and find it out, then I will give you thirty*

linen garments and thirty changes of clothes, but if you cannot tell me what it is, then you shall give me thirty linen garments and thirty changes of clothes." And they said to him, "Put your riddle, that we may hear it." And he said to them,

*"Out of the eater came something to eat.
Out of the strong came something sweet."*

And in three days they could not solve the riddle.

The spirit of the Lord filled Samson with great strength as a roaring lion approached him, and without anything in his hands, he tore the lion into pieces. Some days later, inside of the carcass of the lion he found honey. He told no one of this experience, but he forms a riddle from it. He shared the riddle with the Philistine people for them to answer although he knew that unless they had been there they would not be able to figure it out.

The Philistines said, "Put forth thy riddle that we may hear it."

<u>*Put forth* in the Strong's in this scripture means:</u>	<u>*Riddle* in the Strong's in this scripture means:</u>
☐ To tie a knot	☐ A puzzle, a trick, conundrum
☐ To propound a riddle	☐ Perplexing questions (difficult)
☐ To propose a riddle	☐ Dark saying, hard question, proverb

Since Samson knew they would not be able to guess his riddle, he was provoking and antagonizing the enemy. He bound and tied them in the knot of this difficult perplexing question. The riddle and bet was a set-up being used as the opportunity for him to strike against the Philistine people. However, remember we are not to be opportunity-based, but lifestyle-based. As apostolic governors, our destiny walk and calling should be what provokes and antagonizes our enemies.

In this instance, Samson's personality was one that was playful, charismatic, and a bit cocky. As he shared the riddle, he was interacting with the Philistine people from a place of toying with them for his own personal satisfaction, but not from a place of strategically binding them as his enemies. Although God used this as an opportunity for the advancement of his purposes, Samson did not have this same focus. As we walk in our destiny and calling our focus and vision should always be about God and his agenda. We are never to be striving for our own personal pleasures.

> ***Judges 14:15-20 English Standard Version*** *On the fourth day they said to Samson's wife, "Entice your husband to tell us what the riddle is, lest we burn you and your father's house with fire. Have you invited us here to impoverish us?" And Samson's wife wept over him and said, "You only hate me; you do not love me. You have put a riddle to my people, and you have not told me what it is."*

And he said to her, "Behold, I have not told my father nor my mother, and shall I tell you?" She wept before him the seven days that their feast lasted, and on the seventh day he told her, because she pressed him hard. Then she told the riddle to her people. And the men of the city said to him on the seventh day before the sun went down, "What is sweeter than honey?
What is stronger than a lion?" And he said to them, "If you had not plowed with my heifer, you would not have found out my riddle." And the Spirit of the LORD rushed upon him, and he went down to Ashkelon and struck down thirty men of the town and took their spoil and gave the garments to those who had told the riddle. In hot anger he went back to his father's house. And Samson's wife was given to his companion, who had been his best man.

The Philistine people could not solve the riddle, so they threatened to kill Samson's wife and her father if she did not get the answer for them. Samson's wife wept and pressed him for the answer for seven days. Finally, he told her the answer and she told it to the Philistine people to spare her and her father's life. That same day, the Philistine people told Samson the answer to the riddle and he knew that his wife had told them. Samson was angry and his pride was hurt because he had lost the bet and was probably not used to being out-witted. The spirit of the Lord came upon him and he struck down 30 Philistine men and took their garments to pay off the bet. This became an opportunity for God to use him to kill the Philistine people, but it was not based on him being intentionally committed to walking in his purpose. God's spirit had to rush Samson because his spirit did not consistently abide in him. Samson is a part of the Old Testament when the promise of the Holy Spirit had not yet been released. However, this is not to justify him in not being focused and intentional in fulfilling his purpose. We now have the Holy Spirit, which should be the main source of what empowers us in destiny and our daily lives. The spirit of the Lord should not have to rush upon us to use us opportunely. God's spirit should be living in us and able to use us intentionally and strategically.

> *Judges 15:1-5 English Standard Version After some days, at the time of wheat harvest, Samson went to visit his wife with a young goat. And he said, "I will go in to my wife in the chamber." But her father would not allow him to go in. And her father said, "I really thought that you utterly hated her, so I gave her to your companion. Is not her younger sister more beautiful than she? Please take her instead." And Samson said to them, "This time I shall be innocent in regard to the Philistines, when I do them harm." So Samson went and caught 300 foxes and took torches. And he turned them tail to tail and put a torch between each pair of tails. And when he had set fire to the torches, he let the foxes go into the standing grain of the Philistines and set fire to the stacked grain and the standing grain, as well as the olive orchards.*

Samson went to visit with his Philistine wife, but her father had given her away to be the wife of his best man. He offered Samson his younger daughter, but Samson was angry that his wife had been taken from him and given to another man without his knowledge. Resultantly, Samson planned to attack the Philistines again, but in a new way. This time he sent 300 foxes with flaming torches tied to their tails running through their fields and harvest. Once again antagonizing and provoking the enemy out of retaliation with no strategy.

> ***Judges 15:6-8 English Standard Version*** *Then the Philistines said, "Who has done this?" And they said, "Samson, the son-in-law of the Timnite, because he has taken his wife and given her to his companion." And the Philistines came up and burned her and her father with fire. And Samson said to them, "If this is what you do, I swear I will be avenged on you, and after that I will quit." And he struck them hip and thigh with a great blow, and he went down and stayed in the cleft of the rock of Etam.*

The Philistines found out that Samson was responsible for ruining their fields and as a consequence, his wife and father-in-law are killed by fire. Samson says "If this is what you do, I swear I will be avenged on you, and after that I will quit." His response shows us a few things about him:

- ✓ Because of what has happened to his wife and father-in-law, he makes a vow to avenge them- this is not a vow to the Lord to walk in his

calling against the Philistine people, this is a self-vow
- ✓ His focus is on avenging what has occurred, not truly on the fact that it is his duty and assignment to wreak havoc upon the Philistine people. His focus, motivation, and purpose is misplaced and visionless
- ✓ He is angered, and emotionally stirred to kill them- not destiny and vision driven
- ✓ He vows to quit after he settles the score and ups another one on them. Letting us know that he is doing this to get revenge
- ✓ To Samson this great slaughter of the Philistine people is about him and not about God

Judges 15:9-16 English Standard Version Then the Philistines came up and encamped in Judah and made a raid on Lehi. And the men of Judah said, "Why have you come up against us?" They said, "We have come up to bind Samson, to do to him as he did to us." Then 3,000 men of Judah went down to the cleft of the rock of Etam, and said to Samson, "Do you not know that the Philistines are rulers over us? What then is this that you have done to us?" And he said to them, "As they did to me, so have I done to them." And they said to him, "We have come down to bind you, that we may give you into the hands of the Philistines." And Samson said to them, "Swear to me that you will not attack me yourselves." They said to him, "No; we will only bind you and give you into their hands. We will surely not kill you." So they bound him with two new ropes and brought him up from the rock.

When he came to Lehi, the Philistines came shouting to meet him. Then the Spirit of the LORD rushed upon him, and the ropes that were on his arms became as flax that has caught fire, and his bonds melted off his hands. And he found a fresh jawbone of a donkey, and put out his hand and took it, and with it he struck 1,000 men. And Samson said,

"With the jawbone of a donkey, heaps upon heaps, with the jawbone of a donkey have I struck down a thousand men."

The Philistines went to the land of Judah and raided the Israelites searching for Samson. To save themselves from further retaliation, the people of Judah confronted Samson about his attacks against the Philistine people and turned him over into their hands. His altercations with the Philistine people brought more harm than good for his people. Since his attacks were from an emotional place of anger, rage and need for revenge, they did not have strategy or wisdom.

As the Israelite people turned Samson over, this became another opportunity and destiny moment for Samson to strike and kill more of the Philistine people. In that one altercation, he killed 1,000 men with the jawbone of a donkey. Think of how much more damage Samson could have done to the Philistine people if he had been committed to the vision of God for his life.

Imagine how destructive we can be when we are one with the spirit of God and devoted to his vision for us. Samson killed 1,000 men with the spirit of the Lord rushing him in that moment, how effective can we be with the spirit of the Lord living in us every moment?

> ***Judges 16:1-3 English Standard Version*** *Samson went to Gaza, and there he saw a prostitute, and he went in to her. The Gazites were told, "Samson has come here." And they surrounded the place and set an ambush for him all night at the gate of the city. They kept quiet all night, saying, "Let us wait till the light of the morning; then we will kill him." But Samson lay till midnight, and at midnight he arose and took hold of the doors of the gate of the city and the two posts, and pulled them up, bar and all, and put them on his shoulders and carried them to the top of the hill that is in front of Hebron.*

Samson slept with a prostitute although he was called as a consecrated Nazarite. In this time in history, it was not offensive to the cultural norms for Samson to use the services of a prostitute. Nobody would have thought less of him. What was a violation was his internal "norm" that God had set with the instructions that he had given Samson for his life that made it offensive to God? A lot of believers in this day and age, are using cultural and social norms to set the standards of their behavior while not considering that it is offensive to God.

While Samson was with the prostitute, an ambush was set up around his location to kill him in the morning. When we are out of alignment with the standards of the Lord we are outside of the protection of God, thus we give the enemy an open door to form attacks. At midnight, Samson took hold of the doors of the gate of the city, he pulled the bars and post of the gate up at its base, placed it on his shoulders, and carried it to the top of the hill. They were not expecting him to leave at that time since they planned the ambush for the morning. The way that he carried the gates upon his shoulders to the top of the hill is a depiction that Samson's gift of supernatural strength had been exalted. His strength got him out of the attack, but the gift was not given to him for that purpose. The instructions for him to remain pure and set apart for the purposes of God were not being utilized, and his actions demonstrated that the standards given to him were not important. His strength had become an idol, and the gift had precedence over the purpose of the gift, and the gift giver. We must guard against allowing the fascination and power of our gifts to become more important than God's standards for us. As apostolic governors, God the giver of our supernatural gifts always takes precedence over the gifts themselves. We must understand that the instructions the Lord has given us for our lives are standards that protect our gifts. The standards guard us, and they create a home and acceptable place for the Holy Spirit to reside.

God-gift giver

Standards-gift protector

Gifts- Supernatural protector

Judges 16:4-9 English Standard Version After this he loved a woman in the Valley of Sorek, whose name was Delilah. And the lords of the Philistines came up to her and said to her, "Seduce him, and see where his great strength lies, and by what means we may overpower him, that we may bind him to humble him. And we will each give you 1,100 pieces of silver." So Delilah said to Samson, "Please tell me where your great strength lies, and how you might be bound, that one could subdue you."

Samson said to her, "If they bind me with seven fresh bowstrings that have not been dried, then I shall become weak and be like any other man." Then the lords of the Philistines brought up to her seven fresh bowstrings that had not been dried, and she

> *bound him with them. Now she had men lying in ambush in an inner chamber. And she said to him, "The Philistines are upon you, Samson!" But he snapped the bowstrings, as a thread of flax snaps when it touches the fire. So the secret of his strength was not known.*

After this event with the prostitute and the gates of the city, Samson met Delilah. The Philistines seemed to have become aware of their relationship and took advantage of it to get to Delilah. It is interesting to note that the scripture says that Samson loved Delilah, but it does not say that she loved him. The difference is what created a gap that left her so easily persuaded to be part of the conspiracy. One key to be learned here is that when we use the world to fulfill a love that belongs to God, the world will never love us back in the same way. When our gifts and power become exalted above God, and become idols in our lives, they come from under the covering of God and are exposed to the enemy. When we uncover our gifts to the devil, demonic assignments are released against them. Proverbs 16:18 says, "Pride goes before destruction, and a haughty spirit before a fall."

The Philistines offered Delilah money to seduce Samson and get the secret of his strength so they could overpower him. She agreed to the deal and asked Samson to tell her where the secret of his strength was so that he might be **bound** and **afflicted**. Hmm what an interesting question to ask someone… Right there would have been a red flag!

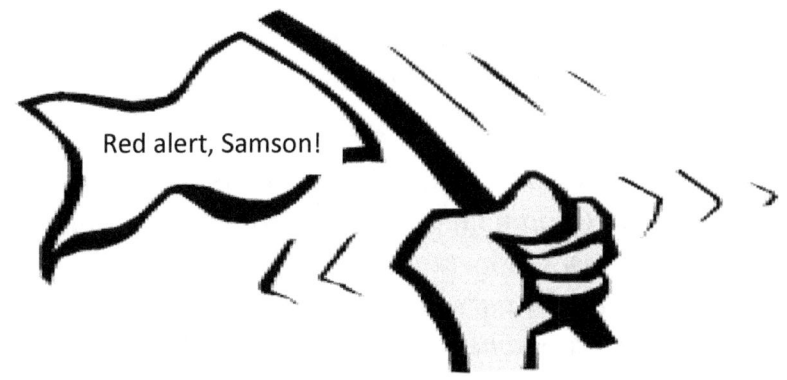

Samson was in a seduced state of love, and from his past experiences we see that he had a weak spot as it pertained to women. Just as his Philistine wife pressed him for the answer to his riddle, Delilah pressed him for the knowledge of the secret of his strength. Because Samson did not have any protection around his gift and who God appointed him to be, he found no need to be cautious concerning Delilah, or the questions that she presented before him. He was not alarmed or triggered by the clear warning signs of the demonic plans of the enemy. We do not lose our gifts when we are in sin because our gifts are given without repentance (Romans 11:29). However, there is a darkness version of our gifts that have been ordained for light. As apostolic governors, we must be discerning, wise, and quick to cautiously protect our gifts and destiny. We cannot be desensitized or have our guards down hindering our ability to pick up on the warning signs of demonic assignments. God, and who we are in God should always take priority over everything and everyone. In the case of Samson, God was not number one; and the fulfilling of his destiny and calling, and following the standards of the Lord for protection was certainly not number one either.

Take a moment and journal what tends to show up in your life when you are out of the will of God. There are weaknesses in us that can be an immediate struggle if we let ourselves be carnal. There needs to be a recognition when the pattern starts forming so we can take proactive measures.

> ***Judges 16:10-17*** *Then Delilah said to Samson, "Behold, you have mocked me and told me lies. Please tell me how you might be bound." And he said to her, "If they bind me with new ropes that have not been used, then I shall become weak and be like any other man." So Delilah took new ropes and bound him with them and said to him, "The Philistines are upon you, Samson!" And the men lying in ambush were in an inner chamber. But he snapped the ropes off his arms like a thread.*
>
> *Then Delilah said to Samson, "Until now you have mocked me and told me lies. Tell me how you might be bound." And he said to her, "If you weave the seven locks of my head with the web and fasten it tight with the pin, then I shall become weak and be like any other man." So while he slept, Delilah took the seven locks of his head and wove them into the web. And she made them tight with the pin and said to him, "The Philistines are upon you, Samson!"*

> *But he awoke from his sleep and pulled away the pin, the loom, and the web.*
>
> *And she said to him, "How can you say, 'I love you,' when your heart is not with me? You have mocked me these three times, and you have not told me where your great strength lies." And when she pressed him hard with her words day after day, and urged him, his soul was vexed to death. And he told her all his heart, and said to her, "A razor has never come upon my head, for I have been a Nazirite to God from my mother's womb. If my head is shaved, then my strength will leave me, and I shall become weak and be like any other man."*

Three times Delilah continued to press Samson to reveal to her the secret of his strength, and each time Samson gives her a false answer. After each answer, he awakes from his sleep to realize he is bound just as he told her, and he breaks free. He does not recognize that Delilah's questions are not idle, or something that she would like to know because she is in a loving relationship with him. She wants to put the secret into action. Instead of Samson acknowledging this and cutting off his relationship with Delilah, he continues to remain in the relationship as she works as a liaison of the Philistines. His relationship with her is an abusive one. She persistently pressures him, binds him, and then makes him feel guilty about it. She was manipulating and weakening him by using emotional and mental witchcraft. She tells him that his heart is not with her and questions his love for her, thus making him self-examine when he was not the enemy. She says, "you have mocked me", but Samson does not confront her and tell her "well you have tried to bind me." He plays with her essentially playing with devil, and playing with the calling on his life. His guard was completely down, as when he realizes he is bound, he is awakening from a place of sleep multiple times. He is caught up in a game with Delilah, and just like he gave the Philistines an impossible riddle to answer, he riddles with Delilah over and over. The scripture says that he was "vexed unto death." This game with Delilah brought him to a place of utter dread and torture. Finally, he breaks and reveals the secret of his strength. Samson played with death, and death won as soon as he revealed the secret of his strength to the enemy.

Keys we learn from this:

- ✓ **Do not play games with the devil!** No matter how smart you are, only using godly wisdom and direction will cause you to outsmart the devil, not your own personal wit, charisma, personality, or intelligence. In playing games with the devil, you form relationship with him and you give him room to play back with you, and he will play back
- ✓ **Do not be blinded to God and truth** when it comes to your relationships such that you are unable to recognize signs of unhealthiness and abuse. You need to be keen to recognize when they are on assignment against you, your standards and purity, your destiny and calling

- ✓ **No person or relationship should take precedence over God** and who you are in Him. You should always have your discernment and wisdom alert and active at all times. No relationship should turn off your discernment and wisdom
- ✓ **Do not sleep on the devils works**, and be desensitized to his tactics
- ✓ **Acknowledge the warning signs** of demonic plans against you, and confront them head on. Do not just push them aside, ignore them, and act like they are normal, or disregard it because it's coming from someone you love. Confront the warning signs before the pressure of all you are not acknowledging breaks you
- ✓ **Never put your guard down** as it pertains to your destiny, calling, identity, and anything that concerns who you are in God. The enemy will see that your guard is down, and he will enter in through that place. Letting your guard down exposes your weaknesses to the enemy. For Samson this was women
- ✓ **Know your weaknesses and give them to God** so that he can fortify and strengthen you in those areas such that when the enemy begins to push against you, you will not break

Judges 16:18-21 English Standard Version When Delilah saw that he had told her all his heart, she sent and called the lords of the Philistines, saying, "Come up again, for he has told me all his heart." Then the lords of the Philistines came up to her and brought the money in their hands. She made him sleep on her knees. And she

> called a man and had him shave off the seven locks of his head. Then she began to torment him, and his strength left him. And she said, "The Philistines are upon you, Samson!" And he awoke from his sleep and said, "I will go out as at other times and shake myself free." But he did not know that the LORD had left him. And the Philistines seized him and gouged out his eyes and brought him down to Gaza and bound him with bronze shackles. And he ground at the mill in the prison.

This time Delilah discerned that Samson had revealed the true secret, so instead of her binding him, she sent for the Philistines. This is detrimental when the enemy has his discernment active but our discernment is compromised. Delilah put him to sleep on her knees and called for one of the men to shave off his locks. She torments him and his strength leaves. Samson is sleep right in the lap of the enemy and is unaware of anything that is happening to him. She bewitches him, as truly when she puts him to sleep and torments him, she strips him of his identity, and sucks out the power of his strength. It was normal for Samson to be sleep in the midst of Delilah, but this normality he created with the enemy bewitched and desensitized him. It became the very thing that trapped him. Samson fell asleep but his enemies did not sleep. What happens when the devil is more watchful than God's called?

Like the times before, Delilah called out to Samson that the Philistines were among him and he says, "I will go out as at other times and shake myself free." He did not realize that his strength was gone. Unfortunately, like in the past God's spirit could not rush upon him and free him. God would supply for the gift to further his purposes, but now that the gift was no longer present, he would not supply for Samson to get out of the obstacle he caused. Samson had woke from his sleep trying to defend himself when he should have already been fortified. He was too late! How long did he think he could play this game and live with a jeopardized gift???

As apostolic governors, we should operate from a place of the offense and never the defense. We must remain ahead and on top of the enemy. Samson thought that he could say and do whatever and that it would cost him nothing. He treated the gift as if it was for him and did not protect it, but the gift was not for him and his personal agendas. His gift was for the saving of his people and was worth being protected and valued. He valued his gift only for the sake of self-gain, but not for its true purpose.

After Samson's strength left him, the Philistines seized him and gouged his eyes out. He had no vision for who he was in the Lord, so as they took his eyes out, it was a natural manifestation of his spiritual condition. There was no protection around his vision so it was easy for the enemy to kill his vision by first cutting his hair, and then utterly destroying any chance he had for vision by taking his eyes.

> ***Judges 16:25-30 English Standard Version***
> *And when their hearts were merry, they said, "Call Samson, that he may entertain us." So they called Samson out of the prison, and he entertained them.*

They made him stand between the pillars. And Samson said to the young man who held him by the hand, "Let me feel the pillars on which the house rests, that I may lean against them." Now the house was full of men and women. All the lords of the Philistines were there, and on the roof there were about 3,000 men and women, who looked on while Samson entertained.

*Then Samson called to the L*ORD *and said, "O Lord G*OD*, please remember me and please strengthen me only this once, O God, that I may be avenged on the Philistines for my two eyes." And Samson grasped the two middle pillars on which the house rested, and he leaned his weight against them, his right hand on the one and his left hand on the other. And Samson said, "Let me die with the Philistines." Then he bowed with all his strength, and the house fell upon the lords and upon all the people who were in it. So the dead whom he killed at his death were more than those whom he had killed during his life.*

After Samson was captured by the Philistines, he became their property. He was their entertainment and they mocked him, laughed at him, played with him like a toy, and utilized him for work. He was likely in captivity for about 2-3 years as his hair had begun to grow back. As he stood upon the pillars he asked the Lord to give him strength one more time to push the pillars down and kill the Philistines for the vengeance of his eyes. There were about 3,000 men and women who were present there. We see here that this is only another opportunity based moment for Samson, as truly he does not say that he wants to kill the Philistines for the sake of his calling which was to save his people. He wants to kill them to get revenge concerning his eyes. Once again he is able to be used against the Philistines. With there being so many people under the structure of the pillars, this was a major advancement against the Philistines. Samson says "Let me die with the Philistines, and he bowed himself with all his might and the house fell upon all the lords, and upon all the people that were therein." He martyred himself for the sake of what the Philistines did to him, but he never genuinely grasped God's true vision for his calling in life from birth. Samson was called from birth to be a Nazarite all the way to the point of his death, but through lack of vision and embrace of the vision, poor life management, and no governing abilities, the fullness of this calling is sadly thwarted. He had to give himself as an unnecessary sacrifice to obtain a moment of strength that God had already designed in him to be life-long.

As we apostolically govern our destiny and calling we should genuinely grasp the vision that God has for our lives. Without vision, we have no clarity of our purpose and what we have to do to attain it. It is key to the successful fulfillment of our destiny that we walk in the standards that God gives us. They are what endue us with power that fortifies our calling.

Without these standards:

- ✓ We are open and susceptible to the enemy
- ✓ We are subject to mistreat our gifts and use them for our own gain
- ✓ We are tempted to sin and have no accountability
- ✓ We can become idols in our own lives where meeting our needs and having our own desires become more important than what God is saying and requiring of us

We must live from the realm of lifestyle-based destiny and be intentional in embodying and fulfilling God's vision.

Prayer:

Decreeing that even now God is giving you clarity on his instructions and standards for your life. Decreeing that he is downloading his blueprint into you concerning the specific vision plan and purpose that he has for your life and the standards that he has for you to protect and fortify his vision for you. As you receive clear vision, I decree that your gifts and abilities are shifting into alignment with the vision that God has ordained for your life and coming out of any places of self- focus, idolatry, and self-gain. Your gifts are being devoted and freshly consecrated to God and his purposes for them. I speak over you today that you will have a destiny journey in the Lord that is destiny lifestyle based and not opportunity based. You will live on purpose in God and be intentional in fulfilling his vision and purposes in you. You will partner with the Holy Spirit, and through his abiding presence in you, you will complete the vision. Because you have keen vision of your destiny and are focused on walking in that vision with God's standards, the enemy will not be able to steal anything from you or thwart your destiny. You will quickly recognize the assignments of the enemy operating against you because your gifts and purposes are being fortified, strengthened, and guarded by your lifestyle that is rooted in the blueprint for your life, so it will be easy to recognize demonic plans. Let God's vision for you be keen and clear to you now. If you already have vision, I decree that it is becoming even clearer and more defined. God's vision is becoming what is most important and prominent in your life, and it will be fulfilled! In Jesus name, Amen.

Chapter 4
Reflection Questions

1. List and journal about the 5 most important points that you have received from this chapter?

2. What clear standards and vision instructions have God given you? In what ways can you walk in these at a greater capacity?

3. Are there areas where your gifts and abilities have been utilized more for you, rather than for their true purpose in God? Journal about this and spend time repenting to God and consecrating your gifts for the purposes of the Lord.

4. In what ways can you be more offensive when it comes to the enemy?

5. Journal about your personal weaknesses. As you spend time in prayer, pray about your weaknesses and allow God to strengthen and fortify you in those places.

6. How can you improve in living from a place of lifestyle-based destiny and not opportunity-based destiny? Make a list of these and write out what steps you plan to take to improve.

Chapter 5

Daniel & His Companions: Excellent Servants Of God

Daniel and his companions Hananiah, Mishael, and Azariah exemplify apostolic governors who embody a spirit of excellence. They were placed in positions of influence within the Babylonian system, yet remained under the subjection and rulership of God. As our destiny and calling leads us to high positions, we must remember who we serve and not be afraid to be vocal about our allegiance to God. Our gifts will make room for us, bring us before great people, and lead us to positions of authority, but we must remain devout in our purpose to advance the kingdom.

> ***Proverbs 18:16*** *A man's gift maketh room for him, and bringeth him before great men.*

God manifested himself through Daniel and his companions because of the godly decisions they made. They were disciplined, consistent, intelligent, learned, and knowledgeable. They understood their identity as set apart pure servants of God. Although they were in high positions of a worldly idolatrous system, they governed as God's agents to assert His influence. Even though in the natural, they were taken to Babylon as captives, they functioned as infiltrators.

<u>*Infiltrate*</u> in Dictionary.com means:

1. To move into (an organization, country, territory, or the like surreptitiously and gradually, especially with hostile intent

2. To pass a small number of (soldiers, spies, or the like) into a territory or organization clandestinely and with hostile or subversive intent.

Infiltrators are like secret soldiers and spies that enter into regions, territories, and worldly systems with the intent to destroy and overthrow that which is not like God. They remain hostile to the environment they are assigned to, and antagonistic to what operates against God. If they begin to be enticed by and conformed to the environment they are infiltrating, they will be hindered in their ability to be an effective infiltrator for God. How can you be hostile toward something you have come into agreement with?? This happens in our society today where those who are called to be voices for God amongst darkness become entangled with the world, and subsequently can no longer be effective or credible voices for God on their platforms. In joining with the world, they become enemies of God.

> *James 4:4 English Standard Version You adulterous people! Do you not know that friendship with the world is enmity with God? Therefore whoever wishes to be a friend of the world makes himself an enemy of God.*

When our destiny and calling positions us to be amid standards and foundations that are not in alignment with God, our stance should be one that is not afraid to have our position, reputation, benefits, and lives jeopardized to bow exclusively to Jesus.

We see this challenge:

- When those in government offices begin their campaign saying that they are for God, but soon after, they begin to promote laws that do not align with God and his word
- In Hollywood, when those who say they are Christian actors with the desire to spread the light amongst darkness, conform to the Hollywood mode and lose their standards
- With Christian singers who take on an ungodly image to "expand" their music to reach the world

Because many have no understanding or revelation about how to govern a calling to these positions of influence, and we may not be called to these positions, many sell out to the idol gods and ruling principalities of these platforms. They become enveloped in the money and benefits, the fame and fortune, the reputation and acknowledgement, and the comfort and security. Eventually, they forsake the call of God altogether. Some believe that they are serving God and are being used by Him even if they have to engage the ungodly requirements of the arena to have influence, but God is not double-minded. He will not call you to purity and consecration and instruct you to compromise. God is not a kingdom divided; either you will serve him or serve the devil. There is no middle ground.

> *Joshua 24:15 And if it seem evil unto you to serve the Lord, choose you this day whom you will serve; whether the gods which your fathers served that were on the other side of the floor, or the gods of the*

> *Amorites, in whose land ye dwell: but as for me and my house, we will serve the Lord.*

<u>Choose</u> in the Strong's in the scripture means:

1. Select
2. Acceptable, appoint, choose
3. Choice, excellent, join, be rather
4. Require, decide, elect, chosen men

Making a choice to only worship God, positions you to be excellent in serving him. The spirit of excellence will keep you disciplined, consistent, intelligent, skilled, devout, and strong in faithfully serving God through the difficulties you may face.

As we study the book of Daniel, we will gain keys on how to govern positions of influence with excellence. It is my prayer that this chapter provide you with revelation that will equip you to advance the kingdom of God as a skilled infiltrator in the midst of darkness.

> **Daniel 1:1-7** *In the third year of the reign of Jehoiakim king of Judah, Nebuchadnezzar king of Babylon came to Jerusalem and besieged it. And the Lord gave Jehoiakim king of Judah into his hand, with some of the vessels of the house of God. And he brought them to the land of Shinar, to the house of his god, and placed the vessels in the treasury of his god. Then the king commanded Ashpenaz, his chief eunuch, to bring some of the people of Israel, both of the royal family and of the nobility, youths without blemish, of good appearance and skillful in all wisdom, endowed with knowledge,*

understanding learning, and competent to stand in the king's palace, and to teach them the literature and language of the Chaldeans.

The king assigned them a daily portion of the food that the king ate, and of the wine that he drank. They were to be educated for three years, and at the end of that time they were to stand before the king. Among these were Daniel, Hananiah, Mishael, and Azariah of the tribe of Judah. And the chief of the eunuchs gave them names: Daniel he called Belteshazzar, Hananiah he called Shadrach, Mishael he called Meshach, and Azariah he called Abednego.

Gain knowledge, insight, & wisdom about the environment of the position you are appointed

The king of Judah had been given over to Nebuchadnezzar the king of Babylon. Daniel, Hannaniah, Mishael, and Azariah of the tribe of Judah were chosen amongst others who expressed qualities that would enable them to stand in the king's palace (a high position). They were "youths without blemish, of good appearance and skillful in all wisdom, endowed with knowledge, understanding learning, and competence." Our qualities of excellence will elevate us where we can be used to implement God's influence. God is raising up youth and millennials who are without blemish. They love holiness, righteous living, purity and godly standards. I am one of them. Contending to live this type of lifestyle impacts me day to day, my relationships, people's perceptions of me, and my destiny. I went through a season where God separated me from friendships that were averse to my destiny. This was not easy at first, but eventually I began to enjoy utilizing the idle time to build a deeper relationship with the Lord. I would worship all day, read all day, pray all day, listen to sermons all day and more. This season of development was setting the foundation for my brand-new life. Now all my relationships reflect a pure and holy lifestyle. God sent people to my life like me who were aiming to walk in destiny, wanted to embody holiness and purity, and had the same standards as me. Some people's perception is that "I do too much" and "it does not take all of that." I have had to learn to be okay with the opinions of others and be at peace with what God has said for me. Everyone will not understand or agree with my lifestyle, but I know my purpose. God uses me as an example of holy living for this generation, and having this knowledge fortifies me through my destiny journey. My consecrated life will influence the lives of others for God's glory.

Daniel and his companions were taught the literature and the language of the Chaldean's and were educated about the background of the native people they were positioned amongst. They gained knowledge about the demonic roots and foundations, thus they were equipped to make godly decisions that would keep them from conformity to the Babylonian system. This is a key because many times we desire high positions that we have no knowledge or background insight about, and we cannot stand against something if we are not aware of its presence. To effectively infiltrate a system for God, you have to be knowledgeable of what you are dealing with such that you can operate with strategic influence and stand against the current rulers of darkness. When you know the culture of the system you can go unrecognized as a threat to their demonic operations.

Many believe that having a relationship with God, and having a general understanding of authority is enough to be successful, but it is not. Passion for people and for influence does not mean we can change people and demonic systems. What we fail to realize is that these systems have been ruled by ancient demonic principalities and powers for years. Therefore, the influence of these demonic powers are rooted in the structure and nature of the environment. It will take more than a basic relationship with God, general understanding, and passion to overthrow principalities and powers. The fulfillment of our destiny and calling will be put in danger if we are not prepared. We have to put work, study, and discipline into learning about where God positions us to sharpen ourselves in skillful excellence. Our level of excellence will be in direct correlation to our level of effective influence.

> ***Daniel 1:8-9*** *But Daniel purposed in his heart that he would not defile himself with the portion of the king's meat, nor with the wine which he drank: therefore he requested of the prince of the eunuchs that he might not defile himself. Now God had brought Daniel into favour and tender love with the prince of the eunuchs.*

Be purposeful, intentional, & determined to keep yourself consecrated & pure to the Lord!

The king appointed a daily portion of meat and drink for those chosen to stand in the king's palace. The scripture says, "But Daniel purposed in his heart that he would not defile himself with the portion of the king's meat, nor with the wine which he drank." Daniel could not eat the king's meat as it was not a part of his consecrated diet. He understood his set apart calling and could not consume what was given to him by the demonic system or partake of what the others could.

<u>Purposed</u> in the Strong's in this scripture means:

1. To put, place, set, appoint, make
2. To set, direct, direct toward
3. To ordain, establish, found, appoint, constitute, determine, fix
4. To be set

He fixed and established in his heart that he would not defile himself by partaking of the king's portion of food. He was purposeful in what he knew he could not do to keep his purity. He constituted a determined plan, and God gave him favor amongst the eunuchs that were set over him.

We have to be purposeful, intentional, and determined in keeping ourselves consecrated to the Lord through all that is presented to us in our positions of influence. We cannot partake of everything that we are exposed to. If it does not line up with God, we have to be bold enough to say no and implement a plan that aligns with what God has said for us. As we uphold ourselves in purity, God will give us favor so that we do not risk our standards. Since I have been called to a life of wholeness in purity, there are certain television shows, movies and music that I cannot partake of. To keep my spirit, soul and body pure, every day I pray for God's presence to cleanse me of things that are not of him that filter in through TV, Facebook, social media, work, conversations, stressful atmospheres and more. I cannot go to clubs, secular parties, or place myself in environments that do not represent my lifestyle in God. I have had to get rid of clothes that held demonic symbolisms, and were too tight or short. God has given me clear vision for what I can and cannot do and where I can and cannot go, because each of these entities should point back to him. There should be no place in my life that he is not Lord over. I have to be intentional in guarding my purity by governing the standards God set for me. Being intentional and having a set plan leaves no room for compromise and grey areas. Sometimes we figure out our standards while we are being faced with decisions and after the fact, but waiting until you are in this position to establish standards will cause you to be persuaded by the position itself, and by the benefits it may seem to have. Daniel was supposed to be given the king's meat and the king's wine; this was the choice food. However, because Daniel was already living out his standards of consecration and purity to the Lord, he recognized the best food concerning Babylonian standards as defilement to his standards.

Not having set and established standards:

- ➢ Will take away your ability to recognize and identify defilement
- ➢ Will cause you to see through your flesh and not your spirit
- ➢ Will sway your decision making, and what looks good at the time will become your standard of the moment
- ➢ Will cause you to eventually mix with the system and be drawn to serving it rather than serving as an infiltrator of God within the system

> ***Daniel 1:10-16 English Standard Version*** *and the chief of the eunuchs said to Daniel, "I fear my lord the king, who assigned your food and your drink; for why should he see that you were in worse condition than the youths who are of your own age? So you would endanger my head with the king." Then Daniel said to the steward whom the chief of the eunuchs had assigned over Daniel, Hananiah, Mishael, and Azariah, "Test your servants for ten days; let us be given vegetables to eat and water to drink. Then let our appearance and the appearance of the youths who eat the king's food be observed by you, and deal with your servants according to what you see." So he listened to them in this matter, and tested them for ten days. At the end of ten days it was seen that they were better in*

appearance and fatter in flesh than all the youths who ate the king's food. So the steward took away their food and the wine they were to drink, and gave them vegetables.

The eunuchs feared if Daniel and his companions did not eat the king's portion of food they would lack in comparison to the others. Daniel persisted that they be given ten days to prove their health would sustain on eating vegetables and drinking water. They found favor with the eunuch and their request was approved. At the end of the ten days they looked better than those who ate the king's portion, so the vegetables and water became their permanent diet. As we commit to the standards of the Lord and are determined to keep them, God will give us favor and honor our dedication. We will not lack in anything, and will always excel those who are in the midst of us but do not serve God.

We are to "be ye separate" and live on the provision of God. As we trust and rely on him, he will be our sustainer and source of support. Our lives should be completely different from those who are in agreement with the demonic system we are infiltrating.

> ***2 Corinthians 6:17*** *Wherefore come out from among them, and be ye separate, saith the Lord, and touch not the unclean thing; and I will receive you.*

<u>Separate</u> in the Strong's in this scripture means:

1. To set off by boundary
2. Limit, exclude, appoint

3. To mark off from others by boundaries, to limit, to separate
4. In a good sense: to appoint, set a part for some purpose

<u>Receive</u> in the Strong's in this scripture means:

1. To take into one's favor
2. To receive kindly, to treat with favour

As we remain separate and consecrated to God, he kindly receives us and treats us with favor. He accepts us, approves of us, and honors our submission to him and his vision of purity for our lives.

> **Daniel 1:17-20** *As for these four children, God gave them knowledge and skill in all learning and wisdom: and Daniel had understanding in all visions and dreams. Now at the end of the days that the king had said he should bring them in, then the prince of the eunuchs brought them in before Nebuchadnezzar. And the king communed with them; and among them all was found none like Daniel, Hananiah, Mishael, and Azariah: therefore stood they before the king. And in all matters of wisdom and understanding, that the king enquired of them, he found them ten times better than all the magicians and astrologers that were in all his realm.*
>
> **Our purity & consecration to God is what makes us excellent!**

God endowed Daniel with understanding in visions and dreams, and gave Daniel, Hananiah, Mishael, and Azariah knowledge and skill in all learning and wisdom. This was God's favor manifesting upon them because they had devoted themselves to being set apart to him. The king communed with all who had been chosen to learn for standing in the king's palace, and amongst all of them none were found like Daniel and his companions. They were unique, distinct, special, favored, and found to be ten times better than the magicians, astrologers, and all that were in the realm of the Kingdom. God was with them, and bestowed them with excellence in every area they learned about. Our knowledge and skill combined with our purity and consecration to God will fill us with qualities that make us excellent.

Daniel 1:20 says, "And in all matters of wisdom and understanding, that the king enquired of them, he found them ten times better than all the magicians and astrologers that were in his realm."

<u>Understanding</u> in the Strong's in this scripture means:

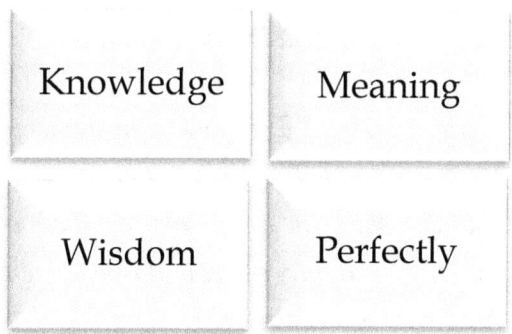

Knowledge	Meaning
Wisdom	Perfectly

God graced them with knowledge, wisdom, meaning, and understanding that was perfect. Having the spirit of excellence allows us to obtain godly perfection.

> ***Daniel 2:1-6 English Standard Version*** *In the second year of the reign of Nebuchadnezzar, Nebuchadnezzar had dreams; his spirit was troubled, and his sleep left him. Then the king commanded that the magicians, the enchanters, the sorcerers, and the Chaldeans be summoned to tell the king his dreams. So they came in and stood before the king. And the king said to them, "I had a dream, and my spirit is troubled to know the dream." Then the Chaldeans said to the king in Aramaic, "O king, live forever! Tell your servants the dream, and we will show the interpretation." The king answered and said to the Chaldeans, "The word from me is firm: if you do not make known to me the dream and its interpretation, you shall be torn limb from limb, and your houses shall be laid in ruins. But if you show the dream and its interpretation, you shall receive from me gifts and rewards and great honor. Therefore show me the dream and its interpretation."*
>
> ***Daniel 2:10-14*** *The Chaldeans answered before the king, and said, There is not a man upon the earth that can shew the king's matter: therefore there is no king, lord, nor ruler, that asked such things at any magician, or astrologer, or Chaldean. And it is a rare thing that the king requireth, and there is*

none other that can shew it before the king, except the gods, whose dwelling is not with flesh.

For this cause the king was angry and very furious, and commanded to destroy all the wise men of Babylon. And the decree went forth that the wise men should be slain; and they sought Daniel and his fellows to be slain. Then Daniel answered with counsel and wisdom to Arioch the captain of the king's guard, which was gone forth to slay the wise men of Babylon:

Handle challenges with good judgement, care, & taste because it will affect your future and the future of others!

The Chaldeans, magicians, astrologers and sorcerers were unable to tell the king his dream, so a decree was made to kill all the wise men. The king did not trust them to interpret the dream if they could not also tell him the dream itself. The wise men were convinced there was no one on earth capable of fulfilling the king's request except for their idol gods who were not of the flesh. The scripture says, "Then Daniel answered with counsel and wisdom to Arioch the captain of the king's guard, which was gone forth to slay the wise man of Babylon."

<u>Counsel</u> in the Strong's in this scripture means:

1. Prudence

Prudent in Dictionary.com is defined as:

1. Wise of judicious in practical affairs; sagacious; discreet or circumspect; sober
2. Careful in providing for the future, provident:

Daniel answered Arioch the Captain of the king's guard wisely with good judgment cautious of the impact his response would have on the future. He addressed the decree of death against him and all the wise men with care and discernment.

We should handle our altercations with wise judgment, understanding that our actions can affect our future. Our responses will provide for our future and the future of others, whether it is good or bad provision. How the situation is handled will unfold some type of consequence. If we had this revelation in our society today, we would see more careful, discreet, and cautious responses in addressing crucial issues.

The scripture also says that he answered with wisdom.

Wisdom in the Strong's in this scripture means:

1. Decree, taste, judgment, command
2. Discretion
3. Report

Taste as it relates to its use in this scripture in Dictionary.com is defined as:

1. The sense of what is seemly, polite, tactful, etc., to say or do in a given social situation.
2. One's personal attitude or reaction toward an aesthetic phenomenon or social situation regarded as good or bad.
3. The ideas of aesthetic excellence or of aesthetically valid forms prevailing in a culture or personal to an individual.

Daniel spoke as decreeing and commanding, addressing the captain with confident power and authority. It is key that wisdom is defined as taste, meaning he responded with good character and integrity. He was polite and appropriate, and did not respond in anger or fear although they were about to kill him and all the wise men. His personal attitude and reaction did not give room for offense or further difficulty. He was tasteful and delicate as he addressed the decree.

Having good character, integrity, and tasteful personal attitudes will either diffuse difficult situations or fuel them. Arioch was seeking Daniel and his companions because he was following the decree of the king to kill all the wise men, so had Daniel responded in a way that was offensive, he could have been killed right there. As he used prudence and taste to address the captain, he gained a chance to go before the king and request that he be given a chance to reveal the dream and interpret it. His response positively affected his future and the future of the other wise men.

> ***Daniel 2:15-18*** *He answered and said to Arioch the king's captain, Why is the decree so hasty from the king? Then Arioch made the thing known to Daniel. Then Daniel went in, and desired of the king that he would give him time, and that he would shew the king the interpretation. Then Daniel went to his house, and made the thing known to Hananiah, Mishael, and Azariah, his companions: That they would desire mercies of the God of heaven concerning this secret; that Daniel and his fellows should not perish with the rest of the wise men of Babylon.*

You need those who will pray, intercede, & cover you in your position!

Daniel gained insight about the decree from Arioch the captain, and was given time to tell the king his dream and its interpretation. He asked his companions to seek God and pray for the revelation of the dream to be revealed so they would not be killed. It is essential to receive prayer and assistance from people who will support and seek God for us when we face threatening challenges. The lack of sufficient support and covering is a major reason why we see many who are in positions of influence fall. They may be surrounded by people who love them, encourage them, and want them to succeed, but are not able to help them adequately govern in their destiny and calling. As God places us on platforms for his influence we need people who will provide sufficient support for the level of challenge we face.

His companions sought the Lord and the interpretation was revealed to Daniel in a night vision. Their prayers pressed for the release of the revelation Daniel needed. Those who pray for and cover us will help us breakthrough to receive what we need.

> ***Daniel 2:19*** *Then was the secret revealed unto Daniel in a night vision. Then Daniel blessed the God of heaven.*
>
> ***Daniel 2:24*** *Therefore Daniel went in unto Arioch, whom the king had ordained to destroy the wise men of Babylon: he went and said thus unto him; Destroy not the wise men of Babylon: bring me in before the king, and I will shew unto the king the interpretation.*
>
> ***Daniel 2:44-47*** *And in the days of these kings shall the God of heaven set up a kingdom, which shall never be destroyed: and the kingdom shall not be left to other people, but it shall break in pieces and consume all these kingdoms, and it shall stand for ever. Forasmuch as thou sawest that the stone was cut out of the mountain without hands, and that it brake in pieces the iron, the brass, the clay, the silver, and the gold; the great God hath made known to the king what shall come to pass hereafter: and the dream is certain, and the interpretation thereof sure.*
>
> *Then the king Nebuchadnezzar fell upon his face, and worshipped Daniel, and commanded that they should offer an oblation and sweet odours unto him. The king answered unto Daniel, and said, Of a*

truth it is, that your God is a God of gods, and a Lord of kings, and a revealer of secrets, seeing thou couldest reveal this secret.

God will use you to release his word & will!

Daniel revealed the dream and interpretation, and king Nebuchadnezzar bowed and acknowledged the God of Daniel. The interpretation of the dream was not about the establishing of the kingdom of Nebuchadnezzar, it was about the establishing of the eternal Kingdom of God that would crush and destroy all other kingdoms. Since the king had no revelation of the true God because he served many idols, when he heard the interpretation he fell on his face and worshipped Daniel as if the word was about the flourishing of his kingdom. The word was about Nebuchadnezzar's kingdom being destroyed and no one even knew it. Daniel was God's hidden infiltrator in the king's palace, releasing his word of truth that was undetectable. His revelation far exceeded the knowledge of any person in the kingdom, but it was secretly paving the way, planting a seed, and creating foundation for the manifestation of the word to go forth.

God will use us to release his word that will be undetectable to those around us. They will receive what we are saying as for their benefit and advancement, but we will be planting a seed and creating an opening for God to infiltrate and establish his will. This is why we cannot be afraid to speak up and release what *thus saith the Lord* because God will protect us by concealing us within the words that we speak. We must speak up, because this is a part of who we are as an infiltrator, and is a way God will use us to have a major influential impact. The seeds we are planting and the influence we are asserting will be a mystery to those who have no revelation.

> ***Matthew 13:11*** *He answered and said unto them, Because it is given unto you to know the mysteries of the kingdom of heaven, but to them it is not given.*

<u>Mysteries</u> in the Strong's in this scripture means:

1. Hidden thing, secret, mystery
2. Secrets confided only to the initiated and not to ordinary mortals
3. A hidden or secret thing, not obvious to the understanding
4. A hidden purpose or counsel
5. Secret will of men, of God: the secret counsels which govern God in dealing with the righteous, which are hidden from ungodly and wicked men but plain to the godly

This realm of knowing is not accessible to those who are not a part of the kingdom of God.

> ***Daniel 2:48-49*** *Then the king made Daniel a great man, and gave him many great gifts, and made him ruler over the whole province of Babylon, and chief of the governors over all the wise men of Babylon.*

God will increase your influence & expand your infiltration!

> *Then Daniel requested of the king, and he set Shadrach, Meshach, and Abednego, over the affairs of the province of Babylon: but Daniel sat in the gate of the king.*

After Daniel revealed the dream and interpretation to the king, he was promoted to chief of the governors over all the wise men. As we speak what God reveals to us he will allow us to be promoted, increasing our influence and expanding our kingdom infiltration. Because of our excellence and the hidden nature of our purpose, we will have favor with those of the system. Daniel requested of the king that his companions also be promoted and set over the affairs of the kingdom. His influential increase gave him the opportunity to elevate his companions who were also set a part to positions where they could also be infiltrators of God in the king's palace. Now that's kingdom infiltration! We should use our influence to help position those who can be effective infiltrators to further God's kingdom agenda.

Daniel appointed Shadrach, Meshach, and Abednego over the affairs of the province, but Daniel sat in the gate of the king.

<u>*Gate* in the Strong's in this scripture means:</u>

1. A door
2. Gate mouth
3. Court
4. A palace

Daniel was a gatekeeper of the kingdom. He was a literal door for God to enter through, and a gate mouth for the entire province. A gate mouth is one who is the epitome of the voice of God. They are the mouthpiece of God and are skilled in administrating, executing, and exercising the power and authority of his voice. Through the gates of their mouths, God releases his word, will, truth, power, and authority, and whatever they speak upon they have the governing influence over. They are not limited to the gates of the regions and territories that they are positioned in. Because their mouth is the gate, they gain charge over whatever they speak over. Through their mouths they had the ability to change, alter, and shift a thing. Due to this very influential power of the gate mouth, it is important that they know how to manage this ability and watch what they say. Many do not know that they are gate mouths and that what they say has great effects on people, their community, their government, and all they speak about.

One way you can identify if you are a gate mouth is by thinking about how the things that you say effect, influence, and change others. You can think about how you are in a group of people, and if your words alter the mood and shift the atmosphere. Another way you can tell is by how much fruit is produced through the things you say. If you are highly influential in the scenarios that I have posed here, you are probably a gate mouth. You have the power and authority to be highly influential through what God shows you and puts in your mouth to speak. Be careful what you release and allow to come through your mouth. You must govern it by keeping it from defilement, consecrating it for the use of God and the advancing of his kingdom. I am a gate mouth, my words have powerful influence on the atmosphere and people around me. At times during my bullying experiences, I would speak very sharply and boldly against the bully's to get the insults to stop. They were used to me responding in a certain way, so when I spoke up they were shocked. They would immediately shut up as I shifted the atmosphere from tension and fear to courage by the power of my mouth. This is when I noticed that my voice had influential power. Therefore, I cannot participate in conversations that are rooted in gossip, slander, perversion or vulgarity. If I say something I should not, I am quick to repent and ask God to cleanse me and others around me who may have been affected by what I said. When venting is necessary, my spiritual family has created what is called "truth day" where we can express our feelings about something. This does not mean I am cursing, engaging in sinful conversation, gossip and offense. It is just a time where I can share the unfiltered truth with trusted people. At the end of this day, we take the time to cleanse from any harsh truths, while making sure to not carry any ungodly emotions of frustration, anger, agitation or more into the next day. By sharing with one another, we can hold each other accountable, and even receive clarity and balance from others who are walking in destiny with us. This helps me govern who I am as a gate mouth and keeps my mouth consecrated for God.

Take a few moments and search out the questions on being a gate mouth for God. Journal about the power of your mouth and the influence it can have for the advancement of God's kingdom.

> ***Daniel 3:1-6 English Standard Version*** *King Nebuchadnezzar made an image of gold, whose height was sixty cubits and its breadth six cubits. He set it up on the plain of Dura, in the province of Babylon. Then King Nebuchadnezzar sent to gather the satraps, the prefects, and the governors, the counselors, the treasurers, the justices, the magistrates, and all the officials of the provinces to come to the dedication of the image that King Nebuchadnezzar had set up. Then the satraps, the prefects, and the governors, the counselors, the treasurers, the justices, the magistrates, and all the officials of the provinces gathered for the dedication of the image that King Nebuchadnezzar had set up. And they stood before the image that Nebuchadnezzar had set up. And the herald proclaimed aloud, "You are commanded, O peoples, nations, and languages, that when you hear the sound of the horn, pipe, lyre, trigon, harp, bagpipe, and every kind of music, you are to fall down and worship the golden image that King Nebuchadnezzar has set up. And whoever does not fall down and worship shall immediately be cast into a burning fiery furnace."*
>
> ***Daniel 3:8-16*** *Wherefore at that time certain Chaldeans came near, and accused the Jews. They spake and said to the king Nebuchadnezzar, O king, live for ever. Thou, O king, hast made a decree, that every man that shall hear the sound of the cornet, flute, harp, sackbut, psaltery, and dulcimer, and all*

kinds of musick, shall fall down and worship the golden image: And whoso falleth not down and worshippeth, that he should be cast into the midst of a burning fiery furnace. There are certain Jews whom thou hast set over the affairs of the province of Babylon, Shadrach, Meshach, and Abednego; these men, O king, have not regarded thee: they serve not thy gods, nor worship the golden image which thou hast set up.

Then Nebuchadnezzar in his rage and fury commanded to bring Shadrach, Meshach, and Abednego. Then they brought these men before the king. Nebuchadnezzar spake and said unto them, Is it true, O Shadrach, Meshach, and Abednego, do not ye serve my gods, nor worship the golden image which I have set up? Now if ye be ready that at what time ye hear the sound of the cornet, flute, harp, sackbut, psaltery, and dulcimer, and all kinds of musick, ye fall down and worship the image which I have made; well: but if ye worship not, ye shall be cast the same hour into the midst of a burning fiery furnace; and who is that God that shall deliver you out of my hands? Shadrach, Meshach, and Abednego, answered and said to the king, O Nebuchadnezzar, we are not careful to answer thee in this matter. If it be so, our God whom we serve is able to deliver us from the burning fiery furnace, and he will deliver us out of thine hand, O king. But if not, be it known unto thee, O king, that we will not serve thy gods, nor worship the golden image which thou hast set up.

Be VOCAL & Make It Clear Who You Serve!

King Nebuchadnezzar had a golden image made and at the dedication of the image he commanded that all people of the provinces bow down and worship the image. The Chaldeans noticed that Shadrach, Meshach, and Abednego were not bowing to worship the golden image so they accused them before the king. King Nebuchadnezzar was angry and said, "Now if ye be ready that at what time ye hear the sound of the cornet, flute, harp, sackbut, psaltery, and dulcimer, and all kind of music, ye fall down and worship the image which I have made." He was giving them another chance to obey the command before being thrown into the fiery furnace. Shadrach, Meshach, and Abednego responded, "We are not careful to answer thee in this matter. If it be so, our God whom we serve, is able to deliver us from a burning fiery furnace, and he will deliver us out of thine hand, O king. But if not, be it know unto thee, O king, that we will not serve thy gods, nor worship the golden image which thou hast set up."

<u>Careful</u> in the Strong's in this scripture means:

1. To be necessary
2. To need, careful, have need of
3. The thing needed

As they told the king they were not careful in answering, they asserted that they did not need another chance to bow. It was not necessary for them to go through the command again because they would not be bowing. They trusted that God would deliver them, but if not, the king was wasting his time because their decision was final and would not be changed. They were deeply devoted to serving God and was willing to give up their lives before they bowed to a false god.

Shadrach, Meshach, and Abednego were willing to lay down everything because God was their source. When the benefits we have become accustomed to are put at risk, we must not live off the position as this will cause us to bow and compromise to protect our comfort.

It is one thing to let your stance speak for you, but is a whole other thing to boldly say no to the devil in the face of death. Currently there is such an increased release of blatant demonic influence, so it is important that we speak up about our allegiance to God if we are influencing people and systems for him. Silence may not necessarily mean agreement, but it leaves room for others to form their own judgments about you because there is no distinctness that you serve God. No one will be influenced for God by you if you give them no clarity of what it means and looks like to serve him.

How can we be effective in being an influence for God if we are not willing to speak up and be clear about serving him? The lack of clarity displays uncertainty about our position in God, and it gives us a chance to ride the fence.

Shadrach, Meshach, and Abednego released an outward confession and declaration of their allegiance to God alone.

- ✓ They did not just ride on the fact that they knew they had a relationship with God and was not in agreement with serving another. They made it known
- ✓ The knowledge of our relationship with the Lord is not enough to stand as infiltrators of God and have powerful influence in demonic systems
- ✓ We cannot just have an inner disposition that we love God, but have no outward declaration of this
- ✓ In fact, if you are truly engaging in a consistent relationship with the Lord and are journeying with him in your destiny and calling, your relationship should be fueling you to stand for him

It should be no secret that you serve God, and that you align your life with him. The people around you should know, see, and hear who you serve. When we are VOCAL, we welcome God's infiltration.

> ***Daniel 3:19-25*** *Then was Nebuchadnezzar full of fury, and the form of his visage was changed against Shadrach, Meshach, and Abednego: therefore he spake, and commanded that they should heat the furnace one seven times more than it was wont to be heated. And he commanded the most mighty men that were in his army to bind Shadrach, Meshach, and Abednego, and to cast them into the burning*

fiery furnace. Then these men were bound in their coats, their hosen, and their hats, and their other garments, and were cast into the midst of the burning fiery furnace. Therefore because the king's commandment was urgent, and the furnace exceeding hot, the flame of the fire slew those men that took up Shadrach, Meshach, and Abednego. And these three men, Shadrach, Meshach, and Abednego, fell down bound into the midst of the burning fiery furnace. Then Nebuchadnezzar the king was astonied, and rose up in haste, and spake, and said unto his counsellors, Did not we cast three men bound into the midst of the fire? They answered and said unto the king, True, O king. He

People will change toward you & and you will go through warfare, but it is powerless against you!

answered and said, Lo, I see four men loose, walking in the midst of the fire, and they have no hurt; and the form of the fourth is like the Son of God.

The scripture says that King Nebuchadnezzar's face was "changed" toward them. In the passages before this, Shadrach, Meshach, and Abednego were favored and elevated over the affairs of the province, but as soon as they defied the demonic principalities and powers of the system, the king changed against them. This is something we need to be aware of and equipped to handle if we are called to high positions. We cannot be wrapped up in pleasing people and avoiding confrontation because in standing for God, people WILL CHANGE against us. When we stand for God, we are also standing against the people who are in agreement with what we are defying. People will be offended and seek to find fault in us to remove and destroy us. They will be angry with us, hate us, persecute us, and aim to destroy us. This does not mean that we are doing anything wrong although it may feel like it. It will also feel like a very lonely and different place, especially if you are one who has walked in continual favor. This is a part of what you will go through as one who is infiltrating a system and being used as a voice of God amongst darkness. We must be fortified to deal with the persecution, the changing of people, the having to stand alone, and the fear of loss so we can keep standing, speaking truth, and trusting God.

The king turned the fire in the furnace up seven times higher, so the men that took Shadrach, Meshach, and Abednego to the furnace were killed by the fire. They were bound in all their garments and then thrown into the fire. Even as we go through challenging situations we will not be stripped or deprived. The devil will not take anything from us. We will stand in the fire fully covered and fortified.

While they were in the fire, the king said "Did we not cast three men bound into the fire?" "But I see four men unbound, walking in the midst of the fire, and they are not hurt; and the appearance of the fourth is like a son of the gods." Shadrach, Meshach, and Abednego entered the fire bound but now they were free walking amid the fire. The devil will think he has us bound, but it is only temporary so God can manifest himself. Although we will be tested by fire, we will be unharmed by its flames.

The king saw that there were four men in the fire and the fourth looked like a son of the gods. The fourth man in the fire was Jesus. He will be there with you in the fire as you endure through persecution and intense warfare. As people change and turn against you, know that Jesus is in the process with you.

> ***Daniel 3:26-30*** *Then Nebuchadnezzar came near to the mouth of the burning fiery furnace, and spake, and said, Shadrach, Meshach, and Abednego, ye servants of the most high God, come forth, and come hither. Then Shadrach, Meshach, and Abednego, came forth of the midst of the fire. And the princes, governors, and captains, and the king's counsellors, being gathered together, saw these men, upon whose bodies the fire had no power, nor was an hair of their head singed, neither were their coats changed, nor the smell of fire had passed on them. Then Nebuchadnezzar spake, and said, Blessed be the God of Shadrach, Meshach, and Abednego, who hath sent his angel, and delivered his servants that trusted in him, and have changed the king's word, and yielded their bodies, that they might not serve nor worship any god, except their own God. Therefore I make a decree, That every people, nation, and language, which speak any thing amiss against the God of Shadrach, Meshach, and Abednego, shall be cut in pieces, and their houses shall be made a dunghill: because there is no other God that can deliver after this sort. Then the king promoted*

> *Shadrach, Meshach, and Abednego, in the province of Babylon.*

The satraps, the governors, the prefects, and the king's counselors witnessed the miracle. God had shown himself to all the high officials and humbled them. Nebuchadnezzar began to bless God and made a command that anyone who spoke against the God of Shadrach, Meshach, and Abednego would be destroyed. Then the king promoted them once again. As we stand for the Lord, go through the process of the fire, and allow God to show himself on our behalf, he will continue to increase and expand our influence. The people of the system will respect and praise our God because of their momentary exposure to him, but do not let your guard down and become familiar with this as it will not last. Stay the course and continue serving God.

Part 1
Study Guide Questions

1. If you know God has called you to be an infiltrator, what things do you think you need to learn about before entering that position to be an effective infiltrator?

2. What set and established plans have God given you? Are you committed to walking in these standards with no compromise? If you do not have any at this time, ask God to reveal them to you. Journal about them.

3. When you are faced with challenges, how do you typically handle them? How can you react in these situations with better character, integrity, taste, and judgement? Remember your response can affect your future and the future of others.

4. How can you be more vocal and distinct about your position in God in a society that is flooded with demonic influence? How can you be more bold and fearless in displaying who you are as a servant of God?

Part 2
Daniel & His Companions: Excellent Servants Of God

Daniel 4:8-18 English Standard Version *At last Daniel came in before me – he who was named Belteshazzar after the name of my god, and in whom is the spirit of the holy gods – and I told him the dream, saying, "O Belteshazzar, chief of the magicians, because I know that the spirit of the holy gods is in you and that no mystery is too difficult for you, tell me the visions of my dream that I saw and their interpretation. The visions of my head as I lay in bed were these: I saw, and behold, a tree in the midst of the earth, and its height was great. The tree grew and became strong, and its top reached to heaven, and it was visible to the end of the whole earth. Its leaves were beautiful and its fruit abundant, and in it was food for all. The beasts of the field found shade under it, and the birds of the heavens lived in its branches, and all flesh was fed from it.*

"I saw in the visions of my head as I lay in bed, and behold, a watcher, a holy one, came down from heaven. He proclaimed aloud and said thus: 'Chop down the tree and lop off its branches, strip off its leaves and scatter its fruit. Let the beasts flee from under it and the birds from its branches. But leave the stump of its roots in the earth, bound with a band of iron and bronze, amid the tender grass of the field. Let him be wet with the dew of heaven. Let his portion be with the beasts in the grass of the earth. Let his mind be changed from a man's, and

let a beast's mind be given to him; and let seven periods of time pass over him. The sentence is by the decree of the watchers, the decision by the word of the holy ones, to the end that the living may know that the Most High rules the kingdom of men and gives it to whom he will and sets over it the lowliest of men.' This dream I, King Nebuchadnezzar, saw. And you, O Belteshazzar, tell me the interpretation, because all the wise men of my kingdom are not able to make known to me the interpretation, but you are able, for the spirit of the holy gods is in you."

Daniel 4:24-27 English Standard Version *this is the interpretation, O king: It is a decree of the Most High, which has come upon my lord the king, that you shall be driven from among men, and your dwelling shall be with the beasts of the field. You shall be made to eat grass like an ox, and you shall be wet with the dew of heaven, and seven periods of time shall pass over you, till you know that the Most High rules the kingdom of men and gives it to whom he will. And as it was commanded to leave the stump of the roots of the tree, your kingdom shall be confirmed for you from the time that you know that Heaven rules. Therefore, O king, let my counsel be acceptable to you: break off your sins by practicing righteousness, and your iniquities by showing mercy to the oppressed, that there may perhaps be a lengthening of your prosperity."*

> *God will use you to overturn demonic ruler-ship!*

King Nebuchadnezzar had another dream and none of the other wise men could interpret it, so Daniel came in. He gave the interpretation that because of the king's sins and oppressions he would be made like a beast for seven periods of time until he reverenced the Most High God as the true ruler of the kingdom. Daniel as the gate mouth of the kingdom released the word of the Lord that overturned the demonic ruler-ship of the king until he bowed and worshipped the one and only true and living God. He influenced the headship of the kingdom, and encouraged the king to stop sinning so that his prosperity could be lengthened. God's purpose as we infiltrate will be twofold, to overthrow the demonic and cause his enemies to acknowledge and reverence him.

> *Daniel 4:28-33 English Standard Version All this came upon King Nebuchadnezzar. At the end of twelve months he was walking on the roof of the royal palace of Babylon, and the king answered and said, "Is not this great Babylon, which I have built by my mighty power as a royal residence and for the glory of my majesty?" While the words were still in the king's mouth, there fell a voice from heaven, "O King Nebuchadnezzar, to you it is spoken: The kingdom has departed from you, and you shall be driven from among men, and your dwelling shall be with the beasts of the field. And you shall be made to*

> eat grass like an ox, and seven periods of time shall pass over you, until you know that the Most High rules the kingdom of men and gives it to whom he will." Immediately the word was fulfilled against Nebuchadnezzar. He was driven from among men and ate grass like an ox, and his body was wet with the dew of heaven till his hair grew as long as eagles' feathers, and his nails were like birds' claws.

King Nebuchadnezzar was boasting about how he built the kingdom in his mighty power for his glory, and while he was saying this, the word that Daniel released came upon him. It was already established in the earth and a voice from heaven spoke and caused it to manifest.

> ***Daniel 4:34-37 English Standard Version*** At the end of the days I, Nebuchadnezzar, lifted my eyes to heaven, and my reason returned to me, and I blessed the Most High, and praised and honored him who lives forever, for his dominion is an everlasting dominion, and his kingdom endures from generation to generation; all the inhabitants of the earth are accounted as nothing, and he does according to his will among the host of heaven and among the inhabitants of the earth; and none can stay his hand or say to him, "What have you done?"
>
> At the same time my reason returned to me, and for the glory of my kingdom, my majesty and splendor returned to me. My counselors and my lords sought me, and I was established in my kingdom, and still more greatness was added to me. Now I, Nebuchadnezzar, praise and extol and honor the King of heaven, for all his works are right

and his ways are just; and those who walk in pride he is able to humble.

At the end of the seven periods of time, Nebuchadnezzar praised, blessed, and honored God. He acknowledged his works as being right and just, and he understood that those who were exalted in pride would be humbled by God. He had been greatly influenced and shifted by what God released and established through Daniel.

> ***Daniel 5:1-9 English Standard Version*** *King Belshazzar made a great feast for a thousand of his lords and drank wine in front of the thousand. Belshazzar, when he tasted the wine, commanded that the vessels of gold and of silver that Nebuchadnezzar his father had taken out of the temple in Jerusalem be brought, that the king and his lords, his wives, and his concubines might drink from them. Then they brought in the golden vessels that had been taken out of the temple, the house of God in Jerusalem, and the king and his lords, his wives, and his concubines drank from them. They drank wine and praised the gods of gold and silver, bronze, iron, wood, and stone.*
>
> *Immediately the fingers of a human hand appeared and wrote on the plaster of the wall of the king's palace, opposite the lampstand. And the king saw the hand as it wrote. Then the king's color changed, and his thoughts alarmed him; his limbs gave way, and his knees knocked together. The king called loudly to bring in the enchanters, the Chaldeans, and the astrologers. The king declared to the wise men of Babylon, "Whoever*

> reads this writing, and shows me its interpretation, shall be clothed with purple and have a chain of gold around his neck and shall be the third ruler in the kingdom." Then all the king's wise men came in, but they could not read the writing or make known to the king the interpretation. Then King Belshazzar was greatly alarmed, and his color changed, and his lords were perplexed.

Belshazzar the son of Nebuchadnezzar was reigning as king following in the prideful foot-steps of his father. He brought the golden vessels that were taken from out of the temple of the house of God for the kings, the princes, his wives, and his concubines to drink wine from. They praised the gods of gold, silver, brass, iron, wood, and of stone. He was defiling what belonged to God and was consecrated for his service. Within that same hour a hand appeared and wrote on the wall of the king's palace. Belshazzar was troubled and he called for the astrologers, Chaldeans, and soothsayers but none of them could translate the message on the wall.

> ***Daniel 5:13-16 English Standard Version*** *Then Daniel was brought in before the king. The king answered and said to Daniel, "You are that Daniel, one of the exiles of Judah, whom the king my father brought from Judah. I have heard of you that the spirit of the gods is in you, and that light and understanding and excellent wisdom are found in you. Now the wise men, the enchanters, have been brought in before me to read this writing and make known to me its interpretation, but they could not show the interpretation of the matter. But I have*

> *heard that you can give interpretations and solve problems. Now if you can read the writing and make known to me its interpretation, you shall be clothed with purple and have a chain of gold around your neck and shall be the third ruler in the kingdom."*

The king acknowledged Daniel as one having understanding, excellent wisdom, light, and the spirit of the gods. He requests Daniel's services and offers him scarlet clothing, a chain of gold, and a promotion to be the third ruler in the kingdom but Daniel refuses his gifts. Although the king recognized his qualities of excellence, he had no revelation of who Daniel truly was as God's infiltrator and mouth gate.

> ***Daniel 5:18-31 English Standard Version** O king, the Most High God gave Nebuchadnezzar your father kingship and greatness and glory and majesty. And because of the greatness that he gave him, all peoples, nations, and languages trembled and feared before him. Whom he would, he killed, and whom he would, he kept alive; whom he would, he raised up, and whom he would, he humbled. But when his heart was lifted up and his spirit was hardened so that he dealt proudly, he was brought down from his kingly throne, and his glory was taken from him. He was driven from among the children of mankind, and his mind was made like that of a beast, and his dwelling was with the wild donkeys. He was fed grass like an ox, and his body was wet with the dew of heaven, until he knew that the Most High God rules the kingdom of mankind and sets over it whom he will. And you his*

> son, Belshazzar, have not humbled your heart, though you knew all this, but you have lifted up yourself against the Lord of heaven. And the vessels of his house have been brought in before you, and you and your lords, your wives, and your concubines have drunk wine from them. And you have praised the gods of silver and gold, of bronze, iron, wood, and stone, which do not see or hear or know, but the God in whose hand is your breath, and whose are all your ways, you have not honored.
>
> "Then from his presence the hand was sent, and this writing was inscribed. And this is the writing that was inscribed: Mene, Mene, Tekel, and Parsin. This is the interpretation of the matter: Mene, God has numbered the days of your kingdom and brought it to an end; Tekel, you have been weighed in the balances and found wanting; Peres, your kingdom is divided and given to the Medes and Persians." Then Belshazzar gave the command, and Daniel was clothed with purple, a chain of gold was put around his neck, and a proclamation was made about him, that he should be the third ruler in the kingdom. That very night Belshazzar the Chaldean king was killed. And Darius the Mede received the kingdom, being about sixty-two years old.

Belshazzar learned nothing from his father's humbling experience and lifted himself in pride against God when he brought the vessels of the temple in to drink wine. Daniel interpreted the writing on the wall and it said that God had numbered the days of his kingdom and was bringing it to an end, that he had been weighed in the balances and found wanting, and that his kingdom was being divided and given to the Medes and Persians. That same night Belshazzar was killed and another was elevated as king. This encounter lets us know that as infiltrators and gate mouths we have massive extents of influential power. God will use us to speak his will and it will come to pass.

> *Daniel 6:1-3 It pleased Darius to set over the kingdom an hundred and twenty princes, which should be over the whole kingdom; And over these three presidents; of whom Daniel was first: that the princes might give accounts unto them, and the king should have no damage. Then this Daniel was preferred above the presidents and princes, because an excellent spirit was in him; and the king thought to set him over the whole realm.*

Once again Daniel's influence in the kingdom continued to increase. He was the first president of the kingdom and was preferred above the other presidents and princes because of his excellent spirit. The king thought to appoint him over the entire realm. Wow! Now that is influence. Daniel was extraordinary, he surpassed those who held the same positions as him and all other officials who were around him. The spirit of excellence will endow us with extreme supernatural abilities to be effective in governing our influence.

> *Daniel 6:4-9 English Standard Version Then the high officials and the satraps sought to find a ground for complaint against Daniel with regard to*

the kingdom, but they could find no ground for complaint or any fault, because he was faithful, and no error or fault was found in him. Then these men said, "We shall not find any ground for complaint against this Daniel unless we find it in connection with the law of his God."

Then these high officials and satraps came by agreement to the king and said to him, "O King Darius, live forever! All the high officials of the kingdom, the prefects and the satraps, the counselors and the governors are agreed that the king should establish an ordinance and enforce an injunction, that whoever makes petition to any god or man for thirty days, except to you, O king, shall be cast into the den of lions. Now, O king, establish the injunction and sign the document, so that it cannot be changed, according to the law of the Medes and the Persians, which cannot be revoked." Therefore King Darius signed the document and injunction.

The devil will aim to find fault in us to accuse us, but our spirit of excellence makes us innocent in the eyes of God!

The other officials were jealous of Daniel, so they looked for a way to accuse him. Because he was faithful to his position and in serving God, they could not find any fault against him. They knew that he was an avid follower of the law of God so they planned to use his relationship with the Lord to set him up. The enemy will use people to accuse us to try to remove us, but because we operate in a spirit of excellence, they will not be able to find any ammo against us. They will result to using what they know about us to set us up. They will use our relationship with God against us to say it is causing us to not follow the commands of the position. When we are set up we must remain faithful and stay committed to God and our relationship with him. We should not stop what we are doing, hide, or compromise. As we keep standing in our devotion and consecration to God, he will cause the trap our enemies set for us to be their own trap. As we learned from Shadrach, Meschach, Abednego and the fire, these attacks have no power over us.

> ***Daniel 6:10-17 English Standard Version*** *When Daniel knew that the document had been signed, he went to his house where he had windows in his upper chamber open toward Jerusalem. He got down on his knees three times a day and prayed and gave thanks before his God, as he had done previously. Then these men came by agreement and found Daniel making petition and plea before his God. Then they came near and said before the king, concerning the injunction, "O king! Did you not sign an injunction, that anyone who makes petition to any god or man within thirty days except to you, O king, shall be cast into the den of lions?" The king answered and said, "The thing stands fast, according to the law of the Medes and Persians, which cannot be revoked." Then they answered and said before the king, "Daniel, who is*

one of the exiles from Judah, pays no attention to you, O king, or the injunction you have signed, but makes his petition three times a day."

Then the king, when he heard these words, was much distressed and set his mind to deliver Daniel. And he labored till the sun went down to rescue him. Then these men came by agreement to the king and said to the king, "Know, O king, that it is a law of the Medes and Persians that no injunction or ordinance that the king establishes can be changed." Then the king commanded, and Daniel was brought and cast into the den of lions. The king declared to Daniel, "May your God, whom you serve continually, deliver you!" And a stone was brought and laid on the mouth of the den, and the king sealed it with his own signet and with the signet of his lords, that nothing might be changed concerning Daniel.

When Daniel found out about the command he immediately went to his house and began to pray. He was disciplined in prayer and prayed three times a day just like he had done before. It was a practice of his life and one that he was not willing to give up to follow the commands of the kingdom. Daniel knew that he could not follow this command and that the only person that could get him through this was God. He did not hesitate about what he should do, he immediately went to the one who he knew had the answer and who would deliver him from the consequences. We must do the same when our devotion to God is tested. Run to him and allow him to be your deliver as you face the traps of the enemy set against you.

The men that aimed to trap Daniel found him praying and told the king so that he would have no choice but to enforce the law he signed. Daniel is favored by king Darius because of his excellent spirit, and the king had his heart fixed on trying to help him. But Daniel is cast into the lion's den and sealed inside.

> ***Daniel 6:18-22*** *Then the king went to his palace, and passed the night fasting: neither were instruments of musick brought before him: and his sleep went from him. Then the king arose very early in the morning, and went in haste unto the den of lions. And when he came to the den, he cried with a lamentable voice unto Daniel: and the king spake and said to Daniel, O Daniel, servant of the living God, is thy God, whom thou servest continually, able to deliver thee from the lions? Then said Daniel unto the king, O king, live for ever. My God hath sent his angel, and hath shut the lions' mouths, that they have not hurt me: forasmuch as before him innocency was found in me; and also before thee, O king, have I done no hurt.*

King Darius was unable to eat or sleep because he was worried about Daniel. God can establish relationship where we least expect it. How many in today's church would condemn Daniel for Darius' concerns for him as if the king's heart for Daniel made Daniel somehow "less than" in his calling. We have to get out of the mode that God will only use people like us to strengthen our calling. At the same time, we have a responsibility of balance and knowing our boundaries with what God is telling us to do. It takes life and experience to operate in that balance. That morning he went to the den and found Daniel still alive. Daniel says, "My God hath sent his angel, and hath shut the lions mouth that they have not hurt me." God was in the den with him and infiltrated on his behalf. God will cause the mouths of our accusers (lions) to be shut and void against us.

Daniel says, "forasmuch as before him innocency was found in me."

<u>Innocency</u> in the Strong's in this scripture means:

1. Purity, innocence, innocence (in God's sight)

Daniel was pure and innocent in the sight of God so this attack had no power and authority to take his life. The devil cannot release judgment against you if you are innocent. Our spirit of excellence in serving God will cause us to be innocent.

> ***Daniel 6:23-28 English Standard Version*** *Then the king was exceedingly glad, and commanded that Daniel be taken up out of the den. So Daniel was taken up out of the den, and no kind of harm was found on him, because he had trusted in his God. And the king commanded, and those men who had maliciously accused Daniel were brought and cast into the den of lions – they, their children, and their wives. And before they reached the bottom of the den, the lions overpowered them and broke all their bones in pieces.*

> *Then King Darius wrote to all the peoples, nations, and languages that dwell in all the earth: "Peace be multiplied to you. I make a decree, that in all my royal dominion people are to tremble and fear before the God of Daniel, for he is the living God, enduring forever; his kingdom shall never be destroyed, and his dominion shall be to the end. He delivers and rescues; he works signs and wonders in heaven and on earth, he who has saved Daniel from the power of the lions." So this Daniel prospered during the reign of Darius and the reign of Cyrus the Persian.*

The king was glad Daniel survived and commanded that the men who accused him be cast into the lion's den. Their children and wives were thrown into the den as well. The trap they set against Daniel became their own trap of death. The king acknowledged God and made a decree that all who dwelled in the dominion of his kingdom should tremble and fear the God of Daniel.

Daniel's influence continued to advance. He was tested and dealt with constant warfare, but he did not compromise his spirit of excellence in serving the Lord. As we apostolically govern embodying excellent service to the Lord, we will have continual favor and promotion. Our influence will be powerful in overthrowing demonic rule and causing people to bow to the only true God. Our excellence will cause the attacks of the enemy to be powerless against us because we will be innocent, pure and immovable in our stance.

Prayer:

Decreeing even now that you are receiving a spirit of excellent servanthood impartation from this chapter. Be filled now with boldness, fearlessness, wisdom, and excellence in standing for the Lord in the midst of darkness wherever he calls you and positions you. Decreeing that you are shifting now in your ability to be completely sold out to God and devoted in his standards, his purity and consecration for your life, and in his vision plan for you. If you do not have a set plan for Gods standards of purity for your life let God begin to speak to you clearly and download his plan and will for your life specifically. Decreeing that as you walk in excellence in serving the Lord and his vision for you none of the attacks of the enemy will overpower you and you will be a powerful demonstrative voice, influence, and infiltrator in the midst of darkness for the kingdom of God! In Jesus name, it is so!

Part 2
Study Guide Questions

1. *Write about who you are as a mouthpiece for God. What are your thoughts about being a mouthpiece? In what ways would you like to grow in this area?*

2. *What does operating in the spirit of excellence look like for you and your personal destiny and calling? What does excellent servanthood to God look like for you?*

3. *How do you influence those around you today? (on your job, in your community, at your school, etc.) In what ways would you like to be more influential?*

4. *When you increase in influence for God, how do you stay away from conforming to the environment you are supposed to be influencing?*

5. *When the enemy is seeking to find fault in you to accuse you, how should you handle this?*

6. *What are five main keys you have received from this chapter? Journal about them as they pertain to your destiny and calling.*

Chapter 6
Governing Yourself As The House Of The Lord

As we have committed to walking in destiny and calling, our entire lives have evolved to being solely devoted to the Lord. Our focus and hearts are set on being all of who God has created us to be and fulfilling our purpose. We have submerged our lives into prayer, worship, fasting, pursuit of greater relationship with the Lord, embodying the nature of his spirit, and producing the fruit of his word and will in all that we do. Our very beings have become the temple of the Lord. Upon initially receiving Jesus as Lord, our lives changed to carry his spirit. However, as we fiercely pursue walking in the fullness of our destiny we have access to an even greater inhabitation because of how we engage and chase after the things of the Lord. We have become his temple and it is crucial that we govern ourselves as his house. The enemy has a desire to steal, kill, and destroy the fruit we create and embody within. This chapter is an applicable deliverance tool you can use to help free yourself from demonic influences operating inside of your temple. You can read the authoritative decree keys aloud for further breakthrough and empowerment!

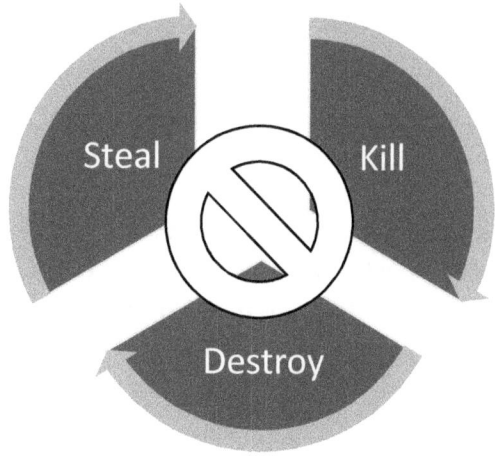

John 10:10 *The thief cometh not, but for to steal, and to kill, and to destroy: I am come that they might have life, and that they might have it more abundantly.*

<u>Steal</u> in the Strong's in this scripture means:

1. To filch, steal
2. To commit a theft
3. Take away by theft
4. Take away by stealth

When the enemy seeks to steal from us he tries to do it covertly such that we do not recognize something is missing, and so we do not try to retrieve what was loss. Patterns of demonic theft will aim to form in us unknowingly and then by the time we become aware of it, much of our fruit and productivity has been stolen. Know that the thief works undercover in the hiding places, but you embody the light of God and can bring quick exposure to the secret works of the enemy. You can overcome it, overtake every enemy, and recover every stolen thing.

> *John 1:5* The light shines in the darkness, and the darkness cannot overcome it.

> *1 Samuel 30:8* Then David asked the Lord, "Should I chase after this band of raiders? Will I catch them?" And the Lord told him, "Yes go after them. You will surely recover everything that was taken from you!"

<u>Kill in the Strong's in John 10:10 means:</u>

1. To sacrifice
2. Immolate (slaughter for any purpose)
3. Kill, sacrifice, slay

The devil wants to sacrifice us, our gifts, calling, destiny, and fruit. He desires to kill us as a sacrifice to himself for his glory and gain. If I never came into the realization that God wanted to use my gift of dance for his glory, my gift would have been exploited in the secular arena with no focus on giving God glory. My gift and the God ordained fruit of my dance would have been sacrificed to the devil. When we utilize our gifts in ways that are not for God's glory, our destinies are being sacrificed (killed), because we are operating outside of genuine purpose for the glory of God, and the advancement of his kingdom. Employing a gift outside of purpose is a sacrifice of worship to the devil whether we acknowledge this or not. Be aware of subtle ways the enemy would try to sacrifice you, your gifts, calling, and destiny for his pleasure. You are a living sacrifice to God. Live as a sacrifice by following all God leads, guides, and directs you to do. As God's temple, this is your reasonable service of worship to the Lord!

> **Romans 12:1** *I appeal you therefore, brothers, by the mercies of God, to present your bodies as a living sacrifice, holy and acceptable to God, which is your spiritual worship.*

<u>Destroy</u> in the Strong's in John 10:10 means:

1. To destroy fully
2. To perish, or lose
3. Die, lose, mar, perish
4. To put out of the way entirely, abolish, put an end to ruin
5. Render useless
6. To declare that one must be put to death
7. To devote or give over to eternal misery in hell
8. To perish, to be lost, ruined, destroyed
9. To lose

The devil desires to destroy us by rendering us useless in who we are and putting an end to us. He will release demonic decree to curse us and abolish our progress. This can hinder us in our health, identity, and relationship with God, desire to live holy, financially, deliverance from sin issues and inner challenges, and more. He will do whatever he can to ruin us, and will manipulate and influence people's lives to sacrifice them to hell.

Jesus came to give us life and life more abundantly.

<u>Life</u> in the Strong's in the scripture means:

1. The state of one who is possessed of vitality or is animate
2. Every living soul
3. Of the absolute fullness of life both essential and ethical, which belongs to God, and through him both to the hypostatic "logos" and to Christ in whom the "logos" put on human nature
4. Life real and genuine, a life active and vigorous, devoted to God, blessed, in the portion even in this world of those who put their trust in Christ, but after the resurrection to be consummated by new accessions (among them a more perfect body), and to last forever.

In Jesus, we have the absolute fullness of life and all that we need to live devoted, active, and vigorous lives. As the enemy plans to steal, kill, and destroy, God's life fills us and overcomes every demonic plan. God always gives us victory, we have overcome by the blood of the lamb and by the word of our testimony, and we are more than conquerors through Jesus Christ.

> ***1 Corinthians 15:57*** *But thanks be to God, which giveth us the victory through our Lord Jesus Christ.*

> ***Revelation 12:11*** *And they overcame him by the blood of the Lamb, and by the word of their testimony; and they loved not their lives unto the death.*

> ***Romans 8:37*** *Nay, in all these things we are more than conquerors through him that loved us.*

We are the temple of the Lord and God is passionate about us.

> **1 Corinthians 3:16** *Do you not know that you are God's temple and that God's Spirit dwells in you?*

> **1 Corinthians 6:19** *Or do you not know that your body is a temple of the Holy Spirit within you, whom you have from God? You are not your own,*

> **Psalms 69:9** *For the zeal of thine house hath eaten me up; and the reproaches of them that reproached thee are fallen upon me.*

> *Good News Translation- My devotion to your temple burns in me like a fire; the insults which are hurled at you fall on me.*

<u>Zeal</u> in the Strong's in this scripture means:

1. Jealousy or envy
2. Ardour, zeal, jealousy
3. Jealous disposition
4. Of God for his people
5. Ardour of anger
6. Of men against adversaries
7. Jealousy resulting in the wrath of God

<u>Up</u> in the Strong's means in this scripture means:

1. To eat
2. Burn up
3. Consume, devour
4. To devour, slay (of sword)
5. Destroy
6. To be devoured consumed of fire
7. To be wasted destroyed

Jesus burns like a demonstrative fire for the temple of the Lord, and he takes personally the insults that come against the temple (you). The anger of the Lord is kindled and unleashed recklessly on your behalf as God's temple. The fire of Jesus's devotion and jealousy for you disintegrates the demonic attacks sent against you. He is personally incited to slay all your oppositions by the sword. As the temple of the Lord, you house God's fire and can use it instrumentally as a weapon of war to destroy your enemies and disintegrate the attacks that come against you.

> **2 Samuel 22:9** *There went up a smoke out of his nostrils, and fire out of his mouth devoured: coals were kindled by it.*

- ✓ Release fire from the mouth of the Lord to devour your enemies and all that is sent against you as the temple.

> **Isaiah 30:30** *And the Lord shall cause his glorious voice to be heard, and shall shew the lighting down of his arm, with the indignation of his anger, and with the flame of a devouring fire, with scattering, and tempest, and hailstones.*

Indignation

1. Rage, raging, storming, anger, wrath

- ✓ Release storms of the rage, anger, wrath, and indignation of the Lord against your enemies.

Flame

1. A flash, a sharply polished blade or point of a weapon
2. Blade, bright, flame, glittering
3. Flame, blade
4. Of flashing point of spear or blade of sword

✓ Release the fiery sharp blade of sword and spear of the Lord to slice and devour your enemies.

Fire

1. Burning, fiery, flaming, hot
2. Supernatural fire
3. Fire (for cooking, roasting, parching)
4. Altar- fire
5. God's anger

✓ Use the supernatural fire and anger of the Lord to roast, parch, and dry up your enemies.

Scattering

1. Driving storm

✓ Scatter your enemies using driving storms of fire.

Tempest

1. A gush of water, flood, overflowing, shower, storm, tempest
2. Rain- shower, thunderstorm, flood of rain, downpour, rain-storm

- ✓ Release flaming thunderstorms and overflowing showers of fiery rain to flood your enemies.

Hailstones

1. A stone
2. Sling, weights, divers
3. Precious stones, stones of fire
4. Stone containing metal, tool for work or weapon
5. Plummet (stones of destruction)

- ✓ Release fiery hailstones of destruction against your enemies.

Isaiah 66:15 For, behold, the Lord will come with fire, and with his chariots like a whirlwind, to render his anger with fury, and his rebuke with flames of fire.

- ✓ Release the fire of the Lord and his chariots to render his furious anger against your enemies. Rebuke them by the flames of fire.

Ezekiel 21:31 And I will pour out mine indignation upon thee, I will blow against thee in the fire of my wrath, and deliver thee into the hand of brutish men, and skilful to destroy.

- ✓ Blow the fire of God's wrath to skillfully destroy and dispel your enemies.

Ezekiel 22:31 Therefore have I poured out mine indignation upon them; I have consumed them with the fire of my wrath: their own way have I recompensed upon their heads, saith the Lord God.

- ✓ Pour out the fire wrath and indignation of the Lord on the heads of your enemies. Recompense their attacks and assaults back onto their own heads. Judge them by fire.

Nahum 1:6-8 Who can stand before his indignation? and who can abide in the fierceness of his anger? his fury is poured out like fire, and the rocks are thrown down by him. The Lord is good, a strong hold in the day of trouble; and he knoweth them that trust in him. But with an overrunning flood he will make an utter end of the place thereof, and darkness shall pursue his enemies.

- ✓ Let the Lord be your stronghold, and release the fire as an overrunning flood putting a complete and utter end to your enemies. Declare that darkness is pursuing your enemies.

The fire wrath, anger, and passion of the Lord is a powerfully destructive spiritual weapon. God is fierce when it comes to you. Who you are as the temple and how God feels about you as his temple is extremely mighty.

John 2:13-17 And the Jews' passover was at hand, and Jesus went up to Jerusalem, And found in the temple those that sold oxen and sheep and doves, and the changers of money sitting: And when he had made a scourge of small cords, he drove them all out of the temple, and the sheep, and the oxen; and poured out the changers' money, and overthrew the tables; And said unto them that sold doves, Take these things hence; make not my Father's house an house of merchandise.

And his disciples remembered that it was written, The zeal of thine house hath eaten me up.

Matthew 21:12-13 *And Jesus went into the temple of God, and cast out all them that sold and bought in the temple, and overthrew the tables of the moneychangers, and the seats of them that sold doves, And said unto them, It is written, My house shall be called the house of prayer; but ye have made it a den of thieves.*

As the people sold and bought in the temple, they were essentially stealing because they were taking away from its true purposes and design. They were robbing the glory, healing, deliverance, and other fruits that were supposed to be produced within the temple. This is the way the devil aims to raid and loot us of what we embody. When the enemy sends demonic attacks against us he is stealing and robbing us of the truth of who we are and what we possess as God's temple. He turns our temple into a playing ground for him and his demonic activity.

<u>Bought</u> in the Strong's in this scripture means:

1. To be in the market place, to attend it
2. To do business there, buy or sell
3. To haunt the market place, to lounge there

As the people were in the temple buying, selling and trading the house of the Lord was reduced to a marketplace. Think of yourself as a marketplace of the enemy… He makes us his own place of business, and because he has set himself in us he is lounging within us. This is the reason why at times it seems like the enemy is always there and like the attacks never end, because the enemy has begun to try to make us his house and place of residence.

When Jesus comes to the temple, his jealous fire is ignited. He goes into the temple and cast all of the thieves out. Jesus has given us this same power to cast out our enemies!

<u>Cast out</u> in the Strong's in this scripture means:

1. To eject
2. Bring forth
3. Drive out
4. Expel, leave, pluck (pull, take, thrust)
5. Put forth, send away
6. To send out with notion of violence
7. To cast out of the world, be deprived of the power and influence he exercises in the world
8. To expel a person from society: to banish
9. To compel one to depart, to bid one depart, in stern though not violent language
10. To command or cause one to depart with haste
11. To draw out with force, tear out
12. With implication of force overcoming opposite force
13. To reject with contempt
14. To draw out, extract
15. To lead one forth or away somewhere with a force which he cannot resist

We can use casting out as a spiritual weapon to expel the attacks of the enemy sent to hinder us. Take a moment to say these decrees out loud.

We cast out every thief spirit that will try to operate in our lives against our destiny and calling!

We eject every thief!

We bring every thief forth and expose it in the light of God and cast it out!

We drive out every thief!

We expel, discharge, and command every thief to exit now!

We pluck, pull up, and thrust out every thief!

We put forth and send out every thief violently, furiously, and impetuously!

We cast the thief out of our life, body, health, destiny path, entire sphere of influence, region, and atmosphere depriving it of all power and influence concerning us!

We cast out every ability of the thief to exercise influence- we make them impotent, weak, lifeless, powerless, null and of no effect!

We compel, bid, and command every thief to depart now quickly with haste in Jesus name!

We draw out and tear out every thief with force!

We reject every thief with contempt, scorn, and disdain!

We lead out every thief with a force that he cannot resist!

The devil cannot resist the power of being cast out in Jesus name!

Jesus overthrew the thieves' tables.

<u>Overthrew</u> in the Strong's in this scripture means:

1. To turn upside down
2. Upset
3. To turn under and over the soil with a plough
4. Throw down

The tables of the money changers are symbolic of demonic exchange tables set up for demonic business. Jesus overthrew and turned over these tables, shutting off the communication lines of the enemy, throwing down his demonic bids and exchanges, and stopping all demonic transactions. We command that every demonic communication and exchange table that is set up in us to be overthrown, turned upside down, plundered with a plough and shut down, ending and canceling all demonic bids and exchanges to steal our fruit and release attacks against us.

Psalms 23:5 says, "You prepare a table before me in the presence of my enemies." This is God's table in us. Even in the midst of our enemies we are able to continue to prosper in the Lord. This table of judgment displays to our enemies that their attacks have no power. God's provision, produce, and communion within us will never be hindered. Even now we overthrow every demonic table of communion and thieving exchange and we receive and establish the feasting and judgement table of the Lord in us.

Jesus also overthrew the seats of those who sold doves.

<u>Seats</u> in the Strong's means:

1. A chair, a seat
2. Used of the exalted seat occupied be men of eminent rank or influence, as teachers and judges

He overthrew the high places and turned over the operations of demonic influence.

> *Philippians 2:9-11* Therefore God has highly exalted him and bestowed on him the name that is above every name, so that at the name of Jesus every knee should bow in heaven and on earth and under the earth, and every tongue confess that Jesus Christ is Lord, to the glory of God the Father.

Jesus rules over all, and all must bow to him. We command that every demonic government, principality, and dark power, be dethroned in Jesus name. We turn over the rank and influence of every demonic agent that is exalting itself above God in our lives. We decree that every exalted seat and high place of the enemy is overthrown and crushed now in Jesus name.

Jesus said "It is written, My house shall be a house of prayer; but ye have made it a den of thieves."

We decree that it is written upon us that we are the house and temple of the Lord. Only the fruits of the spirit, prayer, worship, and constant communion with

God are our portion. We decree now that our temple is no longer a den for thieves and a lounging place for the enemy. Only the attributes of God and his kingdom have the ability to enter and operate in our house.

Den in the Strong's in this scripture means:

1. A cavern
2. A hiding place or resort
3. Cave

The devil tries to hide in secret caves within the temple. A cavern is typically something that is underground such that it remains hidden, in secret, and undetectable. When dens and caverns are formed this means that the enemy has created a place in us to stay, and now that place must be destroyed. He may latch onto things within us like our minds and thoughts, our emotions and hearts, our bodies and health, he will even hide in our blood and generational line. He does this to keep us from discovering the source and origination of the attacks, but like Jesus, we can cast out, throw out, and destroy every secret den of the enemy. How interesting it is that the cavern of the enemy in this scripture was inside of the house of the Lord. The enemy aims to bring effective destruction by infiltrating the most consecrated places in your life and destiny. As we apostolically govern ourselves as the temple of the Lord, we must beware of demonic hiding places. The spiritual weapons and prayer strategies we have gained from this chapter will help us bring utter destruction to demonic infiltrations and operations in our lives.

Prayer:

I decree that even as Jesus entered into the temple and he saw the true nature of the demonic activity that was taking place that you would have that same ability to discern the devil quickly when he tries to infiltrate your temple. I decree that you will be demonstrative, violent, and reckless like Jesus in casting him out and overthrowing him with haste, and every enemy of your temple will run out on fire quickly. Let your eyes and your spiritual senses be as quick and keen as Jesus to see beyond the surface to the root, and point of origination of the demonic activity that is taking place as a means to steal your fruit, and send countless hidden attacks against you. I decree you will be able to pinpoint and locate the source of the attacks quickly and you will cast it out and plough it at its root. Even now we destroy every den, cave, hiding place, lounging place, and resort of the enemy that he has formed in you and we demolish and plunder it now in the name of Jesus. We expose and cast out every demonic latching that the enemy may have formed in your mind and thoughts, your heart and emotions, your body and systems, and your blood and generational line. It is exposed now and there are now no more hiding and lodging places for the enemy in you, your generational line, your region, and your entire sphere of influence. We set every demonic spirit on fire out of Jesus's jealous wrath and anger for you as his temple and the house of his body and spirit. The thief assignments against you are no more, the death assignments against you are no more, the destruction assignments against you are no more today in Jesus name. We decree complete restoration and replenishing of all that has been stolen and hindered by the enemy, and that a gathering and fresh infilling of all the fruit of God in you is your portion in Jesus name. Let continual fruit and increase be your portion in Jesus name as you apostolically govern over yourself as the temple and house of God. In Jesus name, Amen.

Chapter 6
Reflection Questions

1. Are there any patterns of demonic theft that you can identify in your life? For example, weariness, sickness, anxiety and etc.

2. Are any of your gifts or talents being used outside of God's purposes to advance his kingdom and bring him glory?

3. Use the tools given on using the scripture to write a decree that demolishes the enemy's plans against you personally as the house of God.

4. In what ways do you feel the enemy robs you f truth? Journal about this and write about your truths in God.

5. Ask God to reveal to you any places where the enemy tries to hide in you and your life to hinder you. Journal what he reveals to you and use the decrees of the chapter to expose, cast out, and overthrow these places.

Chapter 7
Destiny As A Lifestyle
By Apostle Taquetta Baker

Let's take a moment to dispel misconceptions, misperceptions, impure motives and myths that hinder us from receiving revelation of our destiny and truly committing to walking in a lifestyle of destiny with God.

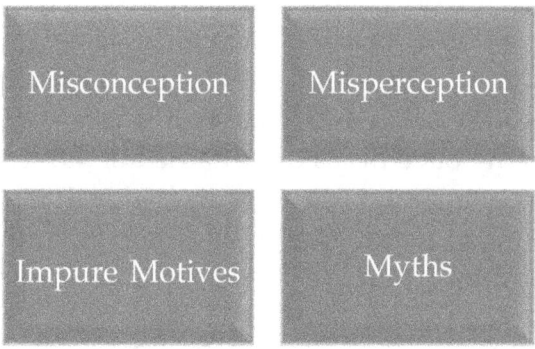

Misconception is a mistaken notion
Misperception is to understand incorrectly
Impure Motives are motives that are unclean, mixed, contaminated, or covetous - the motive is birthed out of lust or focus on self without considering what is best or appropriate for self or for others
Myths are something lived or perceived as true but is more of a fairy tale, fantasy, or lie

Let's first deal with a few misconceptions and misperceptions about destiny:

- Destiny is not necessarily a destination or a goal we are trying to reach, as those points of success are just destiny moments. Destiny however, is a lifestyle of living in the purpose and plan God ordained for us at birth. Destiny is not just a moment with God but a journey in and with God. #SHIFT

- A destiny moment is temporary success. A destiny lifestyle is life time success with constant destiny moments.

- Destiny is not always easy. It requires strategic efficient work to maintain and sustain in destiny. Even people who were handed a destiny moment have to work that moment to maintain a lifestyle of destiny. This is the reason a person keeps working once they have attained or succeeded in a particular area, or to a particular level. They are striving to maintain and sustain in what they have achieved.

   Ephesians 2:10 The Amplified Bible *For we are God's [own] handiwork (His workmanship), recreated in Christ Jesus, [born anew] that we may do those good works which God predestined (planned beforehand) for us [taking paths which He prepared ahead of time], that we should walk in them [living the good life which He prearranged and made ready for us to live].*

   Psalms 139:16 The Amplified Bible *Your eyes saw my unformed substance, and in Your book all the days [of my life] were written before ever they took shape, when as yet there was none of them.*

From these scriptures we recognize that at creation, God already committed to walking in destiny with us.

He made it a part of our DNA, our very substance, and instilled it into the plans for our lives.

This is the reason many people achieve destiny things (money, fame, material goods, temporary happiness, rewards, successes) without God, as he put these talents and gifts in them at birth. Yet despite attainment, many of these people are still unhappy, longing, and constantly searching and filling themselves up with things in effort to acquire fulfillment. This is because true destiny fulfillment can only come through and with God.

Destiny is not necessarily about what we can do or attain as this is a bi-product of destiny. This is the result of destiny.

Destiny is about:

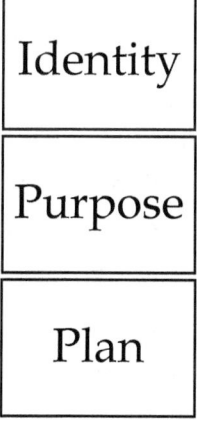

- who we are uniquely in God (Identity)
- why we are to do what he has called us to do (Purpose)
- the reason we are meant to do and be whatever he has chosen us to be in life (Plan)

Jeremiah 1:5 Before I formed thee in the belly I knew thee; and before thou camest forth out of the

> *womb I sanctified thee, and I ordained thee a prophet unto the nations.*
>
> **Isaiah 49:1** *Listen, O isles, unto me; and hearken, ye people, from afar; The Lord hath called me from the womb; from the bowels of my mother hath he made mention of my name.*

So basically destiny is more about:

- What makes you, you?
- What reasons did God make you, you?

Sometimes we are committed to the idea of destiny or the part of destiny that benefits us, but not destiny itself. Our drive to pursue destiny is innate. However, many of us tend to be focused on what we are to do and achieving those goals, rather than the reason we are to do what we do and allowing that to be the drive for attaining our life's desires and goals.

Being driven by what we do rather than the purpose God chose us to do what we are to do, can cause our motives to be distorted, mixed, contaminated, or not in alignment with the committed purposes and plans God instilled in us at creation.

> **Proverbs 20:24** *Man's goings are of the Lord; how can a man then understand his own way?*

Interestingly that word *goings* means *companionship or steps* which insinuates walking with God.

> **Jeremiah 10:23** *LORD, O Lord, I know that the way of man is not in himself: it is not in man that walketh to direct his steps.*

Steps means *goings* and *a course of life*. Jeremiah was saying that man was not designed to walk without God. Man was not designed to do his own thing aside from God.

> **Psalms 37:23** *The steps of a good man are ordered by the Lord: and he delighteth in his way.*

God is invested in the steps – the goings and course of man. So much so that he takes delight – pleasure - in journeying with us. He takes pleasure in helping us to accomplish what he has instilled in us.

Being able to focus on what reason God chose us rather than what we are to attain, has to do with the position and state of our heart.

> **Proverbs 16:9** *A man's heart deviseth his way: but the Lord directeth his steps.*

> **Proverbs 19:21** *Many are the plans in a person's heart, but it is the LORD's purpose that prevails.*

> **Proverbs 16:2-3** *All the ways of a man are clean in his own eyes; but the Lord weigheth the spirits. Commit thy works unto the Lord, and thy thoughts shall be established.*

As I searched the reasons why the scriptures keep cautioning us to resist being redirected by our hearts, I was reminded of **Proverbs 4:23** which states: *Keep thy heart with all diligence; for out of it are the issues of life."* The Amplified bible says "*out of it flows the springs of life.*"

> **Matthew 15:18** *But the things that come out (issue forth) of a person's mouth come from the heart, and*

these defile them. For out of the heart proceed evil thoughts, murders, adulteries, fornications, thefts, false witness, blasphemies: These are the things which defile a man: but to eat with unwashen hands defileth not a man.

Now we all have issues. We are all working on something. We are rarely without a challenge – issue – that requires conquering. Issues derive from unhealed, wounded, hurt, frustrated, sinful, unchallenged or unfulfilled areas within our soul. These areas in turn, affect our emotions and thoughts by distorting the truth of who we are, who God is, and how our lives are to be in him.

Such distortions make our heart unreliable as it causes us to make decisions that are:

> Not the notion of God (misconception)

> Not the perception of God (misperception)

> Not the motive or intent of God (impure motives)

> Not the will of God for our lives (myths and fantasy lifestyles)

When we make decisions with our heart, we veer from a committed destiny walk with God. We end up doing our own thing and consult God more out of convenience than through a committed lifestyle relationship with him. We equate any good, success, and achievements that come from our life to God, even though it is our gifts flourishing in us simply because that is what they have been placed in us to do. Yet we do not recognize that since we are not committed to God, he is not getting any glory out of our lives, nor is his hand upon us or our flourishing giftings. It is like having the essence of God work in you but the presence of God is not there.

> ***Proverbs 16:3*** *Commit thy works unto the Lord, and thy thoughts shall be established.*

Commit in the Hebrew is gâlal:

1. to roll (literally or figuratively)
2. remove, roll (away, down, together), run down, seek occasion, trust, wallow

Dictionary.com defines *roll* as:

1. to move along a surface by revolving or turning over and over
2. to move or be moved on wheels, as a vehicle or its occupants
3. to flow or advance in a stream or with an undulating motion, as water, waves, or smoke.
4. to move as in a cycle
5. to revolve or turn over once or repeatedly

Dictionary.com defines *wallow* as:

1. to roll about or lie in something
2. to live self-indulgently; luxuriate; revel
3. to flounder about; move along or proceed clumsily or with difficulty

These definitions further confirm how God's commitment to destiny is intertwined in us, and how God rolled his purposes and plans into us, where true fulfillment comes from wallowing in life with him. Living a destiny lifestyle in him.

> **Verse 2-3 The Amplified Bible** *All the ways of a man are pure in his own eyes, but the Lord weighs the spirits (the thoughts and intents of the heart). Roll your works upon the Lord [commit and trust them wholly to Him; He will cause your thoughts to become agreeable to His will, and] so shall your plans be established and succeed.*

Thoughts in the Hebrew is *machashebeth* and means:

1. a contrivance (plan or force), i.e. (concretely) a texture, machine, or (abstractly) intention, plan (whether bad, a plot; or good, advice)
2. cunning (work), curious work, device, imagination, invented, means, purpose, thought

Some of the successes, rewards, plans, etc. that we are witnessing in the world are not the destiny of God. God is not committed to them, and they are not the establishment and successes of God. It is the ways of man or the ways of the devil – what man or the devil deems as pure intentions, inventions, devices, workings or achievements. But because it possesses a form of God's grace and blessings – his essence, many of us assume it is of God, and that these ways and lifestyles are the representation of destiny.

> **2Timothy 3:5** *Having a form of godliness, but denying the power thereof: from such turn away.*

That word *form* means *"an appearance or likeness but it also means semblance." Semblance* means *"to have an affinity or attraction to something."* This means we can be drawn into our own way of destiny. Yet in our pursuit, we are left empty or incomplete, because without God, there is no true destiny.

We see many people walking in a form of destiny with lots of power. However, God's power

- possesses his spirit and his fruit - his nature and his character
  (Matthew 7:15-23, 1Samuel 24:13, Luke 6:43-44, Psalms 1:5-6)
- draws people to him (John 12:32)
- transforms lives for the good and betterment of his kingdom and the world as a whole
  (Matthew 10:8, Galatians 6:10, Romans 8:28)

One of the things we must understand about how God created us is whatever gifts and abilities he put in us, they will manifest whether we live for him or not.

> **Romans 11:29** *For the gifts and calling of God are without repentance.*

This scripture reveals that God does not recall his gifts simply because we do not use them for his glory. Whether we use them for him or the devil, they will manifest. However, just because God does not repeal his gifts, does not mean he accepts whatever we do with them. God is clear about serving him or the devil. And though we think we may not be rejecting God when we use our gifts for the devil or without consulting him, he does reject us.

> ***Revelations 3:15-16*** *I know thy works, that thou art neither cold nor hot: I would thou wert cold or hot. So then because thou art lukewarm, and neither cold nor hot, I will spue thee out of my mouth.*

"*Spue*" means to "*vomit up.*" When we vomit our bodies are essentially rejecting whatever it is we took in. Whatever we consumed did not agree with our body system so it regurgitated it. *Lukewarm* means "*indifferent or unconcerned.*" Lukewarm means having no concern about what pleases God as it relates to one's destiny. Many people are this way as they just live life striving to survive and are more focused on paying bills and getting their immediate needs and desires met, as opposed to exploring whether what they are doing in life is the purpose and plan of God. God says because a person is lukewarm in their works – their destiny, he vomits them out of his mouth. He rejects them. His silence, lack of conviction or lack of public judgment does not mean he approves; he has *spued* the person out of his mouth, so there is no need for further dialog. This is because a vomiting mouth does not speak with words, it speaks with sounds of disgust and with a disapproved rejected substance.

The challenge most of us have with destiny is it is not really discussed in our households until we are in high school and are striving to find a path in life. And even then the concern is more about us going to college or getting a job so we can take care of ourselves. There is minimal focus on identifying our purpose and calling. It is God's plan however, that we are cultivated in destiny from the womb, and that we are grounded in his word and purpose concerning who we are to be.

> ***Proverbs 22:6*** *Train up a child in the way he should go: and when he is old, he will not depart from it.*

<u>Train up</u> in the Hebrew *"hanak"* and means:

1. figuratively to initiate or discipline
2. dedicate, inaugurate (induct into office with a formal ceremony or install)
3. to train, train up

In our youth, many of us are placed in sports, dance classes, singing and music lessons, as we are cultivated in some of the talents or things we do well. But even then there is minimal discussion of destiny and truly being inaugurated, inducted, installed, and trained up in our purpose from a young age. Even if we do well in these areas, the focus is more on fame and fortune, rather than the purpose for the fame and fortune, and how God can acquire glory out of our lives. This needs to change in society, especially since much fame and fortune yields to secular and worldly means, which is rooted in the devil and not God.

Even if a person has a Godly upbringing, because they lack revelation of the purpose of their calling, they succumb to the devil's demise. They end up using their gifts to bring the devil glory or to bring themselves glory while calling it God.

This is the reason God says he wish that we were either hot or cold, and not lukewarm. When we are lukewarm we strive to serve two masters, God and the devil, and call it God. Since we are desensitized to truth, we equate our success to God and think we are pleasing and serving him. But whether we discern truth or not, God will not share his glory with the devil. In God's perspective, it is the devil's glory whether we acknowledge that or not.

> ***Matthew 6:24*** *No man can serve two masters: for either he will hate the one, and love the other; or else he will hold to the one, and despise the other. Ye cannot serve God and mammon.*

When God begins to deal with you about destiny, it is important to adhere to what he is speaking. He is striving to SHIFT your life in alignment with him. God knows your destiny and the potential you have. He is striving to align you with it so you will not miss destiny. The challenge with this is while God is speaking, many of us already have our plan and perceived notion regarding what we want to do in life and what our life will be like. Many of us are not willing to relinquish our plan for the plan of God. Or we strive to fit our plan into what God is saying. Neither of these options work as though God will never succumb to our will or desires. We have to surrender ourselves to his will and desires, and then allow him to identify what is of him and what is not of him regarding our plans.

> ***Isaiah 14:24*** *The Lord of hosts has sworn saying, Surely as I have thought, so shall it come to pass; and as I have purposed, so shall it stand:*

Regardless to whether you live out God's plans, they stand. The Lord's plans never change for our lives. What changes is whether we achieve them or not, and whether we live a life of true fulfillment and experiencing real lasting joy in what we do and who we have become.

> ***Psalms 16:11*** *Thou wilt shew me the path of life: in thy presence is fulness of joy; at thy right hand there are pleasures for evermore.*

If you do not experience continual fulfillment and your joy is fleeting and temporary, then check to make sure you are living a life of destiny in God.

Dispelling Destiny Myths

Let's dispels some myths that are more fantasy and fairy tales of destiny, but are not necessarily the truth about destiny.

Though our destiny can entail the following, destiny is not necessarily about:

- Being rich, famous, being well known, having large platforms, an abundance of followers or likes on social media. We can still have fulfilled destiny and never have any of these things.

- Being perfect. We will make mistakes in our destiny walk. If we were perfect we would not need God.

> ***Psalms 37:23-24*** *The steps of a good man are ordered by the Lord: and he delighteth in his way. Though he fall, he shall not be utterly cast down: for the Lord upholdeth him with his hand.*

The key is remaining rooted and grounded in God so he can pull us back into the standard we need to continue our walk of destiny.

> ***New Living Translation*** *The Lord directs the steps of the godly. He delights in every detail of their lives. Though they stumble, they will never fall, for the Lord holds them by the hand.*

> ***The Amplified Version*** *The steps of a [good] man are directed and established by the Lord when He delights in his way [and He busies Himself with his every step]. Though he falls, he shall not be utterly cast down, for the Lord grasps his hand in support and upholds him.*

> ***The Message Version*** *Stalwart walks in step with God; his path blazed by God, he's happy. If he stumbles, he's not down for long; God has a grip on his hand.*

- Pleasing people or being approved by people (Some of the loneliest and most unfulfilled people are the most famous, rich, and popular people) (John 12:43)

Luke 16:15 *And he said unto them, Ye are they which justify yourselves before men; but God knoweth your hearts: for that which is highly esteemed among men is abomination in the sight of God.*

1Samuel 16:7 *But the LORD said to Samuel, "Do not consider his appearance or his height, for I have rejected him. The LORD does not look at the things people look at. People look at the outward appearance, but the LORD looks at the heart."*

1Thessalonians 2:4 *But as we were allowed of God to be put in trust with the gospel, even so we speak; not as pleasing men, but God, which trieth our hearts.*

Colossians 3:22 *Servants, obey in all things your masters according to the flesh; not with eyeservice, as menpleasers; but in singleness of heart, fearing God: And whatsoever ye do, do it heartily, as to the Lord, and not unto men*

- Avoiding hardship or trials or having the easy road in life. There will be trials and tribulations.

2Timothy 2:3-4 *Thou therefore endure hardness, as a good soldier of Jesus Christ. No man that warreth entangleth himself with the affairs of this life; that he may please him who hath chosen him to be a soldier.*

John 16:33 *These things I have spoken unto you, that in me ye might have peace. In the world ye* *shall have tribulation: but be of good cheer; I have overcome the world.*

Psalms 34:19 *Many are the afflictions of the righteous: but the LORD delivereth him out of them all.*

Destiny is about:

- ✓ Commitment
- ✓ Obedience
- ✓ Sacrifice
- ✓ Accountability
- ✓ Impacting the lives of others
- ✓ Impacting the world
- ✓ Glorifying God
- ✓ Being your authentic self – living your God ordained purpose
- ✓ Achieving success while possessing (owning) life
- ✓ Building a heritage that others can gleam from and add to

Mark 12:29-30 *The Amplified Bible Jesus answered, The first and principal one of all commands is: Hear, O Israel, The Lord our God is one Lord; And you shall love the Lord your God out of and with your whole heart and out of and with all your soul (your life) and out of and with all your mind (with your faculty of thought and your moral understanding) and out of and with all your strength. This is the first and principal commandment.*

Everything about you has to be surrendered to God such that you can truly commit and live a life of destiny. You have to love God

- out of and with your whole heart
- out of and with all your soul (your life)
- out of and with all your mind (with your faculty of thought and your moral understanding)
- out of and with all your strength (everything within your being)

Nothing can be more important than pleasing him and making sure he is receiving glory out of every facet of your life.

The Message Version *Jesus said, "The first in importance is, 'Listen, Israel: The Lord your God is one; so love the Lord God with all your passion and prayer and intelligence and energy.'*

Destiny Wisdom Keys

❖ Destiny is not necessarily about having a lot of ideas and huge plans. The most effective people who sustain in destiny have one or a few ideas. They then work that one idea or a couple of ideas into something bigger, impacting, and long lasting. And once they are sustained in a few ideas, they expand into other areas of their destiny.

Matthew 25:23 His lord said unto him, Well done, good and faithful servant; thou hast been faithful over a few things, I will make thee ruler over many things: enter thou into the joy of thy lord.

❖ Even though God's plans for your destiny may not have been part of your life plans or what you considered your destiny to be, if you align with God, you will never resent destiny.

- ❖ Destiny is like an unfolding prophecy. Destiny will pull you toward a truth that does not exist in your present world.

2Corinthians 3:8 *But we all, with open face beholding as in a glass the glory of the Lord, are changed into the same image from glory to glory, even as by the Spirit of the Lord.*

Isaiah 46:10-11 *Declaring the end from the beginning, and from ancient times the things that are not yet done, saying, My counsel shall stand, and I will do all my pleasure: Calling a ravenous bird from the east, the man that executeth my counsel from a far country: yea, I have spoken it, I will also bring it to pass; I have purposed it, I will also do it.*

Isaiah 14:24 *The LORD of hosts hath sworn, saying, Surely as I have thought, so shall it come to pass; and as I have purposed, so shall it stand:*

- ❖ Walking in destiny has a sense of fulfillment to it that does not always make sense to you or others. You and even others will initially speak against certain destiny requirements, because the natural mind cannot comprehend what is unfolding from the spirit. The key is trusting your spirit despite your perceptions and despite the perceptions of others. Trust the vision God is giving and trust him to give you understanding as you journey in destiny with him.

Psalms 138:8 *The LORD will perfect that which concerneth me: thy mercy, O LORD, endureth for ever: forsake not the works of thine own hands.*

John 13:5-7 *After that he poureth water into a bason, and began to wash the disciples' feet, and to wipe them with the towel wherewith he was girded. Then cometh he to Simon Peter: and Peter saith unto him, Lord, dost thou wash my feet? Jesus answered and said unto him, What I do thou knowest not now; but thou shalt know hereafter.*

Jeremiah 4:22 *For my people are foolish, they have not known me; they are stupid children, and they have no understanding: they are wise to do evil, but how to do good they have no knowledge.*

- ❖ Destiny often births something new, so there is no standard of measure. Even if you have similarities of someone or something else, there will always be something unique about who you are and what you are producing that is different from others. This is because each of us hold a unique representation of God, therefore destiny in and of itself has no competitor. Destiny is often attached to an initiative that is new to the world. Just remember that it is not new to God. It was always a part of His plan. The timing of your birth and the development of YOU allowed, "Thy will be done in the earth as it is in the heaven . . . ." With destiny, the history of the world was waiting on YOU to be in place.

2Corinthians 5:17 *Therefore if anyone is in Christ, he is a new creature; the old things passed away; behold, new things have come.*

Isaiah 43:18-19 *Remember ye not the former things, neither consider the things of old. Behold, I will do a new thing; now it shall spring forth; shall ye not know it? I will even make a way in the wilderness, and rivers in the desert.*

Prayer:

Thank you Lord for the destiny of each reader and who you have designed and purposed them to be from the womb. Thank you for every gift that you have placed in them that is appointed to give you glory. Even now we shift out of good gifts and talents, and into destiny, from out of fleeting destiny moments, and allowing our gifts to serve the devil. We repent now and ask your forgiveness of taking of what was ordained for you and using it outside of its design. Cleanse and wash every place where our destinies have become distorted, misaligned, and defiled by the enemy. Cleanse every myth, misperception, and misconception in us about our destiny path and journey. Let your restoration and healing come upon us now. We are being healed in who we are in you, who you are in us, and the truth about our destiny. We shift now to being committed and devoted to walking in the truth of who we are and giving you glory through it, where our lives are a consistent fulfillment of destiny. We receive new joy, new zeal, new love, and new excitement about the journey with you Lord. And we thank you that from the beginning you have committed to walking it out with us.

Thank you Jesus for solidifying these prayers in us and shifting us to a new place of destiny truth and destiny fulfillment. In Jesus name, Amen.

Chapter 7
Reflection Questions

1. What are the misconceptions, misperceptions, and myths you have regarding destiny? (Spend time repenting and cleansing yourself of these negative attributes).

2. What is your motive as you pursue destiny? Are you more focused on surviving or attaining or achieving the purpose to which you were called to attain in life? (Examine yourself and explore this before God).

3. What are some of your heart issues that may affect your decisions as you journey in destiny? (Constantly check yourself in these areas and seek God for deliverance and healing).

4. Is your way of pursuing destiny clean and pure to you but not necessarily to God? Does it line up with the word, standard, and nature of God? (Anything that is of God should be in line with his word and character).

5. Have you asked God how he feels about how you are living your life and whether it is pure in his eyes or whether it aligns with his purposed destiny for your life? If not ask him and make changes as he leads.

6. Do you trust God to lead you in your destiny journey? In what ways do you need to be

healed in the areas of trust to walk with God? Ask God to teach you how to trust him.

> Please know your will is important in your relationship with God. Be willing to give up your way for his, as you will not regret true destiny!

Chapter 8
My Destiny Fulfilled

The concept of fulfilling destiny is significant to me because it emphasizes the fact that there is divine purpose, nature, image, and design intended specifically for me by God. He loved me so much that he took the time to create an intricate plan for the progression of my life well before it began. Why would I leave my life up to chance, when chance becomes concrete with God? And why would I settle for a good life without him, when I can live a fulfilled life with him that will carry over into eternity? When my life shifted in alignment with God's preordained plan for me, destiny became my consistent pursuit. I eat, breathe, and think destiny. It has become my life's consumption as I wholeheartedly aspire to please God and bring him glory through my lifestyle. As I think about my life before this shift, I had great experiences, lots of fun and successes, and enjoyed imagining and creating plans for my future, but there was always something missing. As a young student, I would enjoy all types of music, going to parties, hanging out, and meeting new friends. Yet, the conviction and drawing of the Lord was always near me. Even though my friends were fun, there was something different about me that at the time could not be explained. For a while, dancing professionally was my goal. I trained and trained for years and constantly pushed myself to get better. To practice, I would go to various open auditions, and some would accept me, while others did not. I joined different dance groups and organizations around the city to further train. This was a great asset to my technique and skill as a dancer. Even with all of this, there was still something missing. We can crowd our lives with doing so many great things that it hides the truth of our unfulfillment, yet, there will come a time when it cannot be suppressed any longer. This is what happened to me and I discovered that the emptiness was coming from a place that was tailor made for God and destiny.

One night in college, I came to my dorm after hanging out and I could not rest. All I kept thinking was "I have to go to church, I have to go to church"! The next day was Sunday so I went to church with a friend and from that day I committed to living for Jesus. This shift is where my purpose, identity, definition, and direction for the path of my life began to unfold. My spiritual mother and mentors of my life began to be released to help me as I embarked on this new path. Their presence in my life helped me understand the need for governing my destiny and calling. The practices they engrained into my life such as prayer, study of the word, personal praise and worship, journaling, balance and resting in God, friendship with the Holy Spirit, are now some of my strongest daily governing tactics.

I build my life on the foundation of destiny as a lifestyle, and understand that every decision, move, change, and step I take can and will affect it. Destiny is by no means easy. Hear me well, it is by no means easy. God is always taking me through different processes to shape me, humble me, or teach me something. My character, identity, how I treat people, and handle relationships is always being challenged to make me a better representation of God in the earth. Even through I experience challenges and hardships, there is nothing else I can imagine myself doing besides fulfilling destiny. There is a joy and serenity that comes when you know you are right where you were created to be. When you submit to destiny, you submit to a lifestyle of learning and you position yourself to be constantly perfected. Along the journey, God perfects me so that I can come into the fullness of his original design for me. Sometimes he works on multiple things at once, and other times he hones in on one aspect. No matter what the season is, I have to continue to live in a submitted lifestyle of learning and resting inside of God, while he does the work in me. In my destiny path thus far, that is one my biggest challenges. The way that I constantly pursue growth, aims to exalt itself above God at times. When this happens, I resubmit myself to processing with God and focusing on what I am learning and receiving from Him. With this stance, nothing will be able to hinder and thwart the fulfillment of my destiny. This is a governing tool that I have acknowledged as necessary for my life.

> ***Philippians 1:6 Amplified Version*** *I am convinced and confident of this very thing, that He who has begun a good work in you will [continue to] perfect and complete it until the day of Christ Jesus [the time of His return].*

Like Daniel, who was called to holiness, purity, and righteousness, I stand strong in the standards of the Lord for my life!

Like Nehemiah, who was called to build and not come down, I pioneer and plow in the kingdom work that God grants to my hands. When I endure seasons of warfare against my destiny, I breakthrough with strategic prayer, discernment, wisdom, and staying positioned in God. I do not come down from the ascended place of destiny!

Like Samson, the supernatural strength and power of the Lord rest on my life to wreak havoc on demonic kingdoms. He has given me set instructions for my life that protect my gifts, calling and destiny. Pride and my destiny itself does not supersede God. I always make God first, and I am obedient to his instructions for my life, because they gird me and increase my strength. Because of this, I see constant victory over the enemies that God has called me to destroy!

Like Mordecai and Esther, I know that I am called for such a time as this, so you will not catch me sleeping on destiny. I understand my purpose and the power that is within me. The apostolic governing covenant relationships of my life are built on the foundations of respect, honor, value, submission and obedience. When I make mistakes, my spiritual mother and mentors corrects me in love, and my character is molded even greater in embodying God's glory.

My destiny will be fulfilled!

As you search out your own journey, what are some of the key governing tools God has given you for your life?

I charge you to seek God for your keys and to arise as an apostolic governor of your destiny and calling. Go forth in the unique strategic plan of the Lord for life. Guard who you are and what you have been called to do with the specific tactics that are designed for you. I charge you with wisdom, keenness, discernment, excellence, obedience, submission, strength, heavenly revelation and knowledge that will aid you through the journey, and bring continuous destruction to your enemies. I decree that every assignment granted to your hands will flourish and the entirety of your destiny will be fulfilled. I decree the revelation you have received from this book will flow into your daily life, and be the beginnings of a new foundation for you. You are the apostolic governor of your destiny! Go forth in Jesus name and glory!

References

"Dictionary.com." *Dictionary.com.* Dictionary.com, n.d. Web. 01 June 2017.

"Olive Tree." *The Olive Tree Bible App by Olive Tree Bible Software.* N.p., n.d. Web. 01 June 2017.

Strong, James. *Strong's Exhaustive Concordance of the Bible.* Abingdon Press, 1890. Print

Kingdom Shifters Books & Apparel
Available at Kingdomshifters.com

BOOKS FOR EVERYONE

Healing The Wounded Leader   Kingdom Shifters Decree That Thang

There Is An App For That   Kingdom Watchman Builder On the Wall

Embodiment Of A Kingdom Watchman   Dismantling Homosexuality Handbook
Releasing The Vision   Feasting In His Presence

Kingdom Heirs Decree That Thing   Let There Be Sight

Atmosphere Changers (Weaponry)

BOOKS FOR DANCERS

Dancers! Dancers! Decree That Thang

Spirits That Attack Dance Ministers & Ministries

TEE SHIRTS

Kingdom Shifters Tee Shirt   Let The Fruit Speak Tee Shirt

Releasing The Vision Tee Shirt   Kingdom Perspective Tee Shirt

Stand in Position Tee Shirt   No Defense Tee Shirt

My God Rules Like A Boss Tee Shirt Destiny Blueprint Tee Shirt

CD'S

Decree That Thing CD

Kingdom Heirs Decree That Thing CD

Teachings & Worship CD's

www.ingramcontent.com/pod-product-compliance
Lightning Source LLC
LaVergne TN
LVHW051113080426
835510LV00018B/2023